Biomechanical Principles of Tennis Technique

Using Science to Improve Your Strokes

Duane Knudson, Ph.D.

Racquet Tech Publishing

An imprint of USRSA

Vista, California, USA

Racquet Tech Publishing
(An imprint of the USRSA)
330 Main St.
Vista, California 92084
www.racquettech.com

Library of Congress Control Number: 2005938186

Cover design and illustrations by Kristine Thom
Photos courtesy of USTA High Performance and the International Tennis Federation (ITF)

Printed in the United States of America

ISBN-13: 978-0-9722759-4-1
ISBN-10: 0-9722759-4-0

CONTENTS

4. BIOMECHANICS OF THE FOREHAND 75

5. BIOMECHANICS OF THE BACKHAND 95

6. BIOMECHANICS OF THE VOLLEY 111

Contents

PREFACE

The purpose of this book is to give tennis players knowledge of key concepts of biomechanics so they can make informed decisions about stroke techniques. Tennis players naturally want to maximize performance while minimizing the risk of injury. These are also the two primary goals of research in sport biomechanics.

The book is not intended to replace your tennis pro. Most certified tennis professionals have some training in the application of biomechanics to tennis strokes. This book will help you interact with your pro/coach to make wise decisions about adjustments to your game. Tennis pros will likely help you integrate the information in this book with the strategic (match plan) and tactical (specific implementation of strategy) knowledge this book does not cover. This book will also help tennis pros and coaches update their knowledge on the mechanics of strokes. Reference citations are provided for key papers, sources, and as tips to readers interested in additional information. I encourage all readers to explore these excellent sources. I apologize to some of my peers whose work could also be cited to support many points, but all supporting data would be a distraction to most readers.

Considerable research has been done on tennis strokes and other striking sports that allows for the creation of a few general principles of tennis mechanics. Tennis mechanics includes the biomechanics of stroke production and the mechanics of ball flight. This book is your introduction to these principles. On the way I will discuss examples of how you apply these principles in an injury prevention program and improving your strokes. There will also be integration boxes because biomechanical knowledge should not be applied separate from the context of the performer, task, or situation. Integration, Advantage, and Stroke Technique boxes provide links to how biomechanics can be integrated with other sport sciences or factors to improve our understanding of the game. Let's get started!

I would like to thank Crawford Lindsey and Kristine Thom of Racquet Tech Publishing and the United States Racquet Stringers Association for their valuable contributions to the book. Some of the application boxes and nice features of this book are due to their fine suggestions. There are also many tennis scientists, coaches, and physicians who have been very generous in sharing their data and expertise with me. Space does not allow me the opportunity to thank all of them individually, but they have my sincere gratitude.

BIOMECHANICAL PRINCIPLES OF TENNIS TECHNIQUE

"A common trait of recreational players is that they try to do things with their hands to make up for their lack of quickness and positioning with their feet as they hit the ball." – Arthur Ashe

Any meaningful discussion of variations of tennis stroke technique requires knowledge of sport biomechanics. Biomechanics is the field of study that focuses on understanding the motion and causes of motion of living things. Sport biomechanics, naturally, focuses on how humans create a wide variety of movements in sports. Fortunately for the tennis player and coach, there is a large body of research on the biomechanics of tennis movements. From the footwork to move on the court, to the adjustments in the stroke to create topspin, biomechanics is an essential tool for understanding movement in tennis.

This text will not revel in the details of this research and its limitations, but will be concerned with painting a picture of the consensus of this body of knowledge that can be applied to tennis. It is easy for biomechanical analyses to churn out hundreds of thousands of numbers representing the time varying values of a myriad of force and motion variables. What is more important, and more difficult, is the identification of key variables that are most influential and interpreting how they affect performance or injury risk. (See Advantage Box 1.1 for a brief discussion of the differences between the levels of scientific evidence and coaching opinion.) Often the biomechanical research supports the experiential wisdom of tennis coaches, but at times the research points to interesting and counterintuitive ideas. This is not surprising given the complex mechanical properties of biological tissues, the complexity of the muscu-

Chapter One

Advantage Box 1.1: Tennis Opinion and Science

Much of tennis teaching on technique is based on the professional experience of coaches. Over time this coaching opinion often tends to converge on the truth, but it also can become stranded on incorrect theories or in controversy. Different coaches often have different opinions about stroke techniques and how to best teach tennis strokes. The major weaknesses of this professional craft knowledge are its lack of control of factors that are influential and the small, systematic sample of persons a professional interacts with. All coaches are not created equal. Coach A with one year of experience with primarily beginners likely has less complete knowledge than Coach B who has ten years of experience with a wide variety of players.

Scientific research, including biomechanical studies, can provide more objective evidence. The controlled conditions of scientific research help ensure that the theories or mechanisms being examined are the only factors that are acting. All scientific knowledge, like experiential knowledge, is not created equal. Some kinds of studies or evidence are stronger than others in establishing a causal link between some technique and injury occurrance or performance enhancement. To give you an idea about the general rules or hierarchy of evidence used in medicine and science, consider the following tennis example.

Suppose a tennis coach believes that young players should not be taught open stance forehands because he believes it could overload the players' arms and shoulders. This legitimate position is based on logic (growing long bones and less muscular strength of young people combine for a smaller safety factor than adults) and a philosophy of player development. In looking at the scientific support for this opinion we will work backwards from the strongest evidence back down toward the professional opinion.

The best kind of evidence would be a randomized, double-blind, long-term prospective study. Unfortunately, there are none of these studies on this topic and there will likely never be any. The practical demands of these studies make them prohibitive in tennis because they take many years, are very expensive, and would require players/coaches to select preferred stroke technique at random and not by their preference. There is also an ethical limitation that would not allow a study to run to expose players' to a hypothesized higher injury risk if there were no major benefits that outweighed this risk.

The next level of evidence could be a retrospective study of adult players. A study looking at injury rates and biomechanical variables of adults grouped by what forehand they primarily played with as youngsters would be quite interesting. The problem is that any differences between these could not be directly attributed to the stroke issue of interest, there could be other factors in our samples or their playing experiences that contributed to any differences in injury or technique observed.

Most biomechanical studies would be at a third level of evidence where the muscle activation, forces, or motions used during the open and square stance forehands are compared. These studies are typically done in samples of adult players. Applying the results of these studies to children is a more indirect use of weak evidence. Even if adults were to use forces or motions near the maximum injury-producing values, it would not be known if young players had the same behavior. Specific studies on young players would be needed, and once this was done scientists would still weigh this evidence in light to some major limitations. First, is the sample of players generalizable to all young players? Second, is this evidence confirmed by similar studies? Third, because this is descriptive data, we do not know if this really does pose a greater risk of injury until prospective studies document injury rates in many players.

In summary, it is common for the media and some people to claim that the latest study proves this or that. This is a misunderstanding of how science builds knowledge from the consensus of a large body of evidence that have various levels of quality and meaning. In complex areas of human performance such as tennis science, there will always be a gap between the working or coaching opinion and what can be supported by scientific evidence.

loskeletal system, and the high-speeds of the game that make most aspects of the movements truly invisible to the naked eye.

Fortunately, much of the fascinating and complex nature of movement in tennis can be easily understood using general principles of biomechanics. Biomechanics scholars have proposed nine or ten generic principles of biomechanics in human movement (Knudson, 2003a). This book is based on six of these principles that are most relevant to tennis (Figure 1.1). These principles of tennis mechanics focus attention on key mechanisms of body movement (biomechanics) and ball trajectory in tennis. The trajectory principles may initially appear to be strictly mechanics (physics) with limited interaction with the biological properties of the tennis player. However, we will see that the biological factors (skill, strength, anatomical motion) do affect the range of speed, spin, and initial trajectories that tennis players can create.

Knowing what body motions were used and how they were created and may be modified are powerful tools for improving performance and reducing the risk of injury in tennis. This chapter will provide a brief introduction to these principles. These principles will underlie much of the discussion on the biomechanics of tennis strokes and movements that are explored in the rest of this book.

 Knowing what body motions were used and how they were created and may be modified are powerful tools for improving performance and reducing the risk of injury in tennis.

FORCE AND TIME

The Force and Time Principle says that motion of any body can be modified by the application of force(s) over a period of time. Most tennis movements are characterized by large forces applied for a short time as opposed to smaller forces applied over a longer time. This principle may be the most important because it deals with the creation or modification of motion. For example, a tennis player rushing the net usually performs a split-step to create reaction and friction forces from the ground to redirect his body to intercept a passing shot. We will see later that the split step employs a coordination and transfer of energy strategy as well as the mechanical properties of muscles to redirect the body in the very short time available to react to the ball.

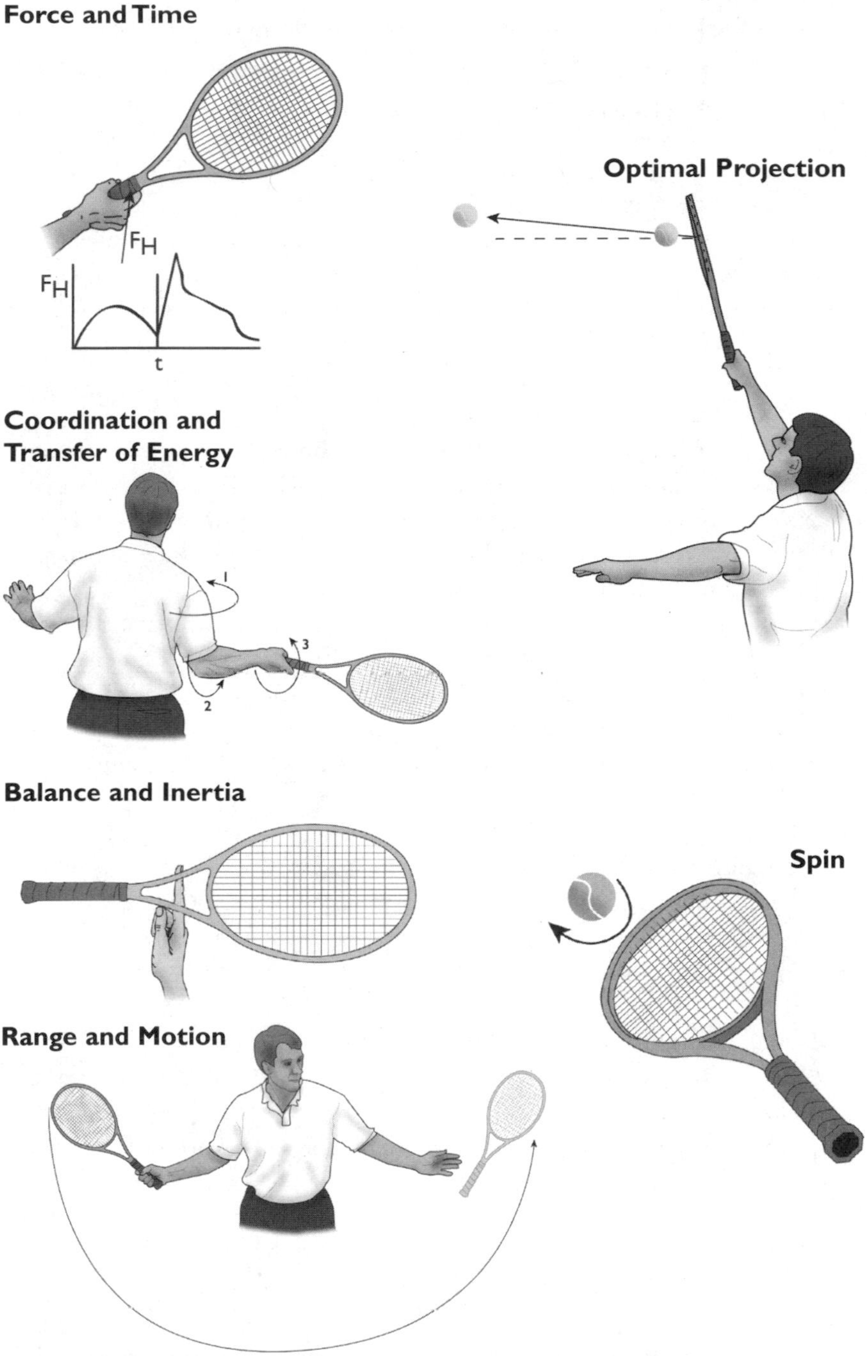
Force and Time
F_H
F_H
t
Optimal Projection
Coordination and Transfer of Energy
1
2
3
Balance and Inertia
Spin
Range and Motion

Figure 1.1 *The biomechanics of tennis will be examined using six principles—four related to body movement and two related to shot outcome.*

Most tennis movements are characterized by large forces applied for a short time as opposed to smaller forces applied over a longer time.

To fully understand and apply this principle, the tennis player needs to understand several key concepts related to force and motion. Many readers will notice that this principle is the direct application of one of the most important laws of physics—Newton's Second Law of Motion. This law is important because it shows the relationship between the forces that cause motion and the resulting motion. Newton originally defined this relationship using both force and time variables (impulse-momentum), but this equation can be rearranged to give the more famous formula ($\Sigma F = ma$) that shows the relationship for any instant in time. The formula—$\Sigma F=ma$—says that the acceleration a body experiences is equal to the sum of the forces in that direction and is inversely proportional to the mass of that body. Two ideas are necessary to fully understand this relationship. The first is that force (F) and acceleration (a) are vector quantities, meaning that they are described by both a magnitude and a direction. Second, the mass of an object is the measure of resistance to change in state of linear motion (speed or direction). This fact is embodied in Newton's First Law, called the Law of Inertia, which states that bodies tend to maintain their state of motion, and the linear measure of this property is simply mass. Because a tennis player cannot decrease his body mass during a point, if he wants to move quickly to the right in our split step example, he must create large ground reaction forces in that direction (Figure 1.2). There is very little time to apply forces, so the forces created must be large. As we will see, the split step is essential to helping the leg muscles create larger forces than they could from a static start.

The example in Figure 1.2 also illustrates another subtle concept about forces. Forces represent the push/pull interaction between two bodies. This is the essence of Newton's Third Law of Motion—for every force, there is an equal force acting in the opposite direction from the other body. Notice that the player in Figure 1.2 pushes with his legs to the left, to create reaction forces to the right. Since the mass of the player is much less that the mass of the court/earth, the reaction force from the ground creates a visible change in velocity (acceleration is the rate of change of velocity) of the player, but not of the earth.

Newton's Second Law and the Force and Time Principle can also be applied in rotations. Forces applied off-center on a body create a tendency to rotate called

Figure 1.2 *A tennis player must create large forces against the ground down and to the left to create large (several times your body weight) ground reaction forces up and to the right to overcome the inertia of his body in moving out of a split-step.*

a moment of force or torque. Torque is dependent on both the force (size and direction) and the right angle distance between the force and the axis of rotation (Figure 1.3).

The resistance to rotary motion or angular inertia is called the moment of inertia. The moment of inertia of objects depends primarily on the location of the mass relative to the axis of rotation. The sum of the mass of each piece of the object times its distance (moment arm) from the axis of rotation is the resistance of that object to rotation about that axis and is known as the moment of inertia. This is commonly called the "swingweight" of a racquet, but it is important to remember two things: objects (such as racquets) typically have different moments of inertia in different planes of motion because shape and mass are not uniform, and objects really have an infinite number of swingweights because you can grip and rotate them at different points (see the book by Cross and Lindsey (2005) for more on the many "weights" of a racquet).

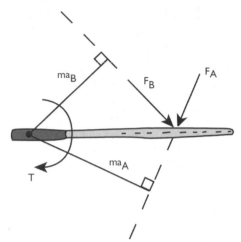

Figure 1.3 *The force of ball impact creates a torque (rotary effect) about the grip. The size of the torque (T) is the product of the force and the moment arm. Note the moment arm does not have to be the length of the racquet, but is the right angle distance between the axis of rotation and the line of action of the force.*

If you want to create greater rotation in a stroke, you must either create greater off-center forces in a short time in the direction you want to rotate, or you must apply smaller forces over a longer amount of time. The tactical situation will dictate the optimal biomechanical strategy to accomplish your aim. You can also decrease the extension in a series of joints to decrease the moment of inertia of your body, so the lower inertia will be accelerated more by the torque you create.

If you want to create greater rotation in a stroke, you must either create greater off-center forces in a short time in the direction you want to rotate, or you must apply smaller forces over a longer amount of time.

COORDINATION AND TRANSFER OF ENERGY

The Coordination and Transfer of Energy Principle is concerned with the origins of the forces that modify motion. External forces represent the interaction of the body with the outside world, while internal force represent the interactions of the segments of the body. A good way to express this principle is that the body creates an external force through a complex coordination and transfer of ener-

Advantage Box 1.2—Transfer of Energy in the Body

A major area of study in mechanics relates to the work done by forces moving objects, and the mechanical energies and power flows in that motion. Unfortunately, most of this experience is in systems much less complex that the human body. The human body has multiple muscles that perform the same joint action, muscles that cross multiple joints, energy storage and release mechanisms, and complex interactions among the three-dimensional motions within and between segments. All these problems, and more, do not currently allow us to uniquely track the transfer of energy in tennis strokes.

Let's begin with an example of apparently passive transfer of energy in strokes. Begin a demonstration of this effect by pinching the grip of your racquet between your thumb and a finger with just enough pressure to suspend the racquet vertically below your hand. Gradually speed up your hand forward and then suddenly slow it and note how your hand motion transferred to the racquet, initially as a inertial lag in the racquet and then as a quick acceleration of the racquet forward. If you move(d) your hand along a line between your fingers, you see little motion in the racquet but great strain on your fingers. In one situation you are able to transfer energy from your arm to racquet motion, while in the other the energy is dissipated in your fingers, which would be analogous to ligaments, bone, or opposing muscles.

We know that much of the energy to rapidly accelerate a racquet late in the serve (Figure 1.4) must come from the lower body because the upper extremity cannot generate this by itself without good Coordination and Transfer of Energy from the lower body. We currently don't have the computing and theoretical knowledge necessary to account for all the sources of energy and how they can be transferred or dissipated in a complex 3D-movement such as the tennis serve. This does not mean we don't know it exists and is extremely important.

gy between the various linked segments of the body. In other words, we can apply large forces to a tennis racquet because we can transfer mechanical energy from the ground through the legs, through the trunk, and up through the arm. This transfer is a very complex phenomenon because muscles have effects beyond the joints they cross and because force acting across joints can transfer energy. Mechanical energy is the ability to perform work on an object by virtue of position in space, motion, or recovery from deformation. Advantage Box 1.2 provides several examples of the transfer of energy between the segments of the body in tennis.

We can apply large forces to a tennis racquet because we can transfer mechanical energy from the ground through the legs, through the trunk, and up through the arm.

In some tennis instruction circles it has become common to talk about the linked system of body segments as a "kinetic chain." This is an adaptation of engineering mechanics terminology (used to simplify modeling and calculations) that begins to create confusion when used to classify movements as either "open" or "closed." A kinetic chain is said to be "closed" if there is significant restraint at both ends. Some would say the arm action in a push-up exercise is a closed kinetic chain because the ground and the body are significant restraints at each end of the chain formed by the hand, forearm, and upper arm. An open chain would be the segments of the opposite arm in a forehand because there is no significant restraint (force or heavy object) at the hand, with only significant restraint at the other end (shoulder joint). It is not clear if the mass of a tennis racquet is small enough to say that weight force of the racquet can be neglected to say the stroking arm in a forehand is essentially an "open" chain motion.

More important than vague classifications of linked segment systems is the concept that the causes of observed motion are often distant from what appear to be obvious sources. The large forces a player can apply to a racquet near the "backscratch" position in the serve primarily originate in the lower leg drive, hip, and trunk rotation (Figure 1.4). Because of the body's linked segment system, forces at one segment can have effects at all the other segments. Biomechanics has only started to develop two-dimensional models of the body to begin to understand how to track the distant effects of a force through a complex linked-segment system (Zajac and Gordon, 1989; Zajac et al. 2002), and the physical meaningfulness of these transfers is controversial (Chen,

Figure 1.4 *Much of the large forces used to accelerate the forearm and racquet (F_E – elbow force) out of the "backscratch" position in the serve comes from the transfer of energy from the legs and trunk.*

2006). The complexity of the human body makes it exceedingly difficult to track the flow of mechanical energy throughout the body in three-dimensions, so documenting exactly how mechanical energy is transferred from the lower extremity to the racquet may only be possible in the future. Coaches need to understand that current use of the kinetic chain concept might communicate the important issue of transfer of energy and source of stroke power distant from high-speed motion, but it certainly is not a scientific theory with any explanatory power.

 Because of the body's linked segment system, forces at one segment can have effects at all the other segments.

Many tennis coaches may base their technique suggestions on a theory of how certain body segments individually contribute to the force used to accelerate the racquet. It is good for a player to understand the theory or philosophy his coach is using. We will see in the rest of this book that biomechanics research has only provided a few tentative answers to many of these coaching/teaching issues. The primary research problems are the great complexity of the body, three-dimensional nature of most tennis movements, variability, individual differences, and a lack of funding for applied tennis research. Only a consensus of several research studies using a variety of biomechanical evidence (motion, forces, theoretical modeling, muscle activation, etc.) can provide answers to important teaching and coaching issues.

What we do know about coordination of segments and the transfer of energy between them are some general trends. First, novices or people with weakness or injury tend to use fewer body segments and poorly coordinate their sequencing. As skill increases more segments can be used and with greater consistency. Second, there is a coordination continuum ranging from nearly simultaneous motion of body segments to more sequential segment motions. The larger the external resistance in a movement, the more simultaneous the motion of the body segments, and the more speed in the movement, the more sequential will be the segment motions. For example, moving a large resistance like the whole body in a split step tends to use simultaneous flexion and extension motion in the lower extremities. A tennis racquet provides a small resistance, so trunk and arm coordination in most strokes is sequential action from the core of the body outward. Third, even though there seem to be common patterns in the movements of players, there is also variation across and within players.

The larger the external resistance in a movement, the more simultaneous the motion of the body segments, and the more speed in the movement, the more sequential will be the segment motions.

The terminology used in kinesiology (the whole academic study of human movement, not just biomechanics) to describe this commonality and diversity in movements ranges from the general to the specific. Classes of movements with a similar pattern (primarily due to biomechanics) are called fundamental movement patterns. An overarm throw or walking are fundamental movement patterns. Specific adaptations of a fundamental movement pattern for a particular objective is a skill. A tennis serve is a sport skill that is a refinement of an overarm throwing fundamental movement pattern. Skills also have variations to suit particular, often tactical, objectives that are called techniques. The slice and twist serve are techniques of a tennis serve. Variation in movement due to the individual is typically related to style. A unique style a particular player has in a technique (e.g., rhythm, kind of backswing) should not be considered an error unless it violates the principles of biomechanics. A longer, lower backswing would be a stylistic feature of a serve which typically would be consistent with the principles of biomechanics and the demands of the shot.

Of course there is much more to the study of human movement variation than trying to determine the difference between a true common tennis technique and a stylistic variation. In fact, recent kinesiology research suggests that variation in many movements, body loading, or practice stimuli may be important to promote health and learning. Tennis players certainly know that a skilled, tough opponent can adjust his game to a variety of shots. Coaches need to realize that the technique adjustments they explore with their players need to be selected within the context of the consistency or variability of the strengths or weaknesses they observe. It is tempting for some to use biomechanics to label some technique points as incorrect. This rather rigid interpretation of the Coordination and Transfer of Energy principles should be avoided. The more you learn about the biomechanics of strokes, the more you realize how much the benefits or limitations of certain techniques are variable and contextual.

BALANCE AND INERTIA

Balance is the ability to control body motion and it is critical in a sport with high body movement and accuracy requirements such as tennis. *The Balance and Inertia Principle states that tennis players must seek the best compromise between motion and stability that suits the situation.* This is critical because stability and mobility in a structure are inversely related. A very wide base of support tends to increase stability, but it also decreases the ability of a person to move his center of gravity beyond the limits of the base in order to run.

Inertia is the body's or segment's tendency to maintain its state of motion, or said differently, to resist changes in its state of motion. Newton realized that all objects have this important property. (See Integration Box 1.1 for further discussion of inertia.) Balance is the ability to control body motion, and this involves controlling its inertia and the forces that effect that inertia. Some posi-

The Balance and Inertia Principle states that tennis players must seek to find the best compromise between motion and stability that suits the situation.

tions or motions require greater or lesser forces than others to change that motion or position. Each shot situation requires a different mix of stability and motion. Good balance is required in both static (or quasi-static) and dynamic situations. The sliding forehand and the serve are examples of quasi-static balance. Executing a split-step or backpedaling to hit an overhead are examples of movements that require balance in more dynamic conditions.

The body postures and stroke techniques a player uses affect both the precision of his movement and the resulting trade-offs between stability and mobility. For example, a player's sliding motion for a wide backhand on clay (Figure 1.5) utilizes a wide base of support that favors stability in order to gradually slow down and maintain balance as opposed to a quick recovery. Research on the quickest footwork and readiness positions is summarized in the groundstroke and volley chapters.

Figure 1.5 *The wide base of support in sliding into strokes on a clay tennis court actually favors stability over mobility, a good compromise because of the unsure footing and slower play on clay courts.*

Integration Box 1.1

Complexity of Inertia

Inertia is the physics term referring to an object's resistance to changes in state of motion. Recall that in linear motion the measure of this inertia is mass. The inertial resistance to rotation is the moment of inertia and depends more on the distribution of mass. Inertia must be overcome to modify motion, but can also be an ally when the desired motion is achieved. Inertia also interacts with the biological and external factors to affect human motion, so knowledge about inertia must be integrated with other knowledge. For example, logic would suggest that decreasing racquet mass would make the frame easier to accelerate. There is a point, however, where this may be counterproductive for most players for several reasons. First, the inertia that is the resistance to racquet speed in the stroke becomes an important inertial resistance to the shock wave of impact. Second, muscle has mechanical properties that make it weaker the faster the muscle is shortening, so

you can have objects with such small inertia that it strongly affects the coordination and how muscles can be used. Image trying to throw two balls, one is a metal shot and the other is a giant ping pong ball. The very low inertia of the large ping pong ball does not allow you to generate much force on the ball before it tends to accelerate out of your grip, therefore you must adopt a sequential coordination strategy to delay the acceleration of the ball to just before release. Third, in most human movements psychological factors have an affect on how movement is perceived. Player's likely have a preferred feel for their racquet, so changes in racquet mass may not feel "right" and affect initial efforts to change racquet properties. A player using a new lighter (lower mass) racquet might take several weeks to consistently be able to create higher-speed strokes with their typical accuracy because of the coordination issues introduced by the lower inertia frame.

RANGE OF MOTION

Closely related to coordination and the timing of force application is the range of motion used by a tennis player. Range of motion is the overall linear or angular distance body parts travel to create a movement. Range of motion is the biomechanical principle that corresponds to what seems to be easily observed by coaches. *The Range of Motion Principle states that there is a continuum of distance traveled by a body part and the number of parts used between low-effort/high accuracy movements and maximum effort/high speed movements.* Decreasing the number of body segments and the extent of their motion will increase the accuracy of the movement (Figure 1.6a). Using many body segments over large arcs of motion safely creates high segment speed at the end of the linked segment system (Figure 1.6b).

(a)

Figure 1.6 *The accuracy of putting away an easy finishing volley is improved by using limited range of motion of few body segments (a), while greater range of motion of more body segments are needs to create high racquet speeds in a groundstroke or serve (b).*

(b)

Acknowledging these generalizations concerning range of motion is important to understanding when one stroke or movement strategy is more effective than another. As we discuss this topic in the various strokes, there will be general guidelines based on what most skilled/elite tennis players do. Like the principle of coordination and transfer of energy, it is not possible to exactly define an optimal range of motion that should be used for the strokes for a particular tennis player. Range of motion is a key concern when a tennis player has a clear flexibility imbalance (see Integration Box 1.2).

The Range of Motion Principle states that there is a continuum of distance traveled by a body part and the number of parts used between low-effort/high accuracy movements and maximum effort/high speed movements.

OPTIMAL PROJECTION

The Optimal Projection Principle states that there are "windows" of optimal initial trajectories for tennis strokes. The predictable effects of the forces of gravity and air resistance, combined with the geometry of a tennis court, make it possible to determine the angles of projection of tennis shots that will land in the opposite court. Players and coaches with knowledge of these "windows or margins for error" can modify strokes to increase their chances of achieving certain tactical objectives during play.

Three computer models have been developed to predict tennis ball trajectories from initial conditions (Brody, 1987; Cooke et al. 2003; Dignall et al. 2004). Unfortunately, there has not been much research directed at validating their predictions with experimental data of actual tennis players. There is secondary support for some of the predictions of these computer models from other tennis biomechanics papers that report some related racquet and ball trajectory data. For example, the Brody (1987) model predicts a player hitting a flat (very little spin) groundstroke from the baseline around 50 mph can typically place the ball in the court if the initial ball trajectory is between 8 and 16 degrees above the horizontal (Figure 1.7).

The Optimal Projection Principle states that there are "windows" of optimal initial trajectories for tennis strokes.

Integration Box 1.2

Kinematics: Measuring Motion

Biomechanists wanting to study the coordination or range of motion used in tennis play usually use high-speed film or video to measure the kinematics (speeds, angles, distances) of actual players. The high speeds of the body and ball in tennis usually require cameras that take 100 to 500 pictures per second. Study of the details of impact require cameras that take 2,000 to 10,000 pictures a second or higher! Special cameras, set-up, scaling, synchronization, and mathematical (calculation and processing) procedures are all required for the measurements made from pictures to be accurate. The high cost of the equipment, software, and time in data processing has limited the number of studies of the three-dimensional motion of tennis strokes. Some "coaching" software programs that allow the storage, replay, and instant measurement (length and angles) on video images on the computer from regualr video should be used with caution. A single video image represents a two-dimensional and distorted picture of three-dimensional objects. Only motions parallel to the video image will be faithfully represented in the image and scaling will depend on the object s distance from the camera. Coaches and players need to keep this in mind when observing tennis strokes. The observer needs to view the stroke from several vantage points to be able to accurately assess all the joint motions used.

Clinicians (physical therapists, athletic trainers, orthopaedic surgeons) also measure joint motions to test flexibility and for the integrity of ligaments that hold joints together. An important area of flexibility for many players is in the hamstring muscles. The hamstrings are the muscles on the back of the thigh that, because they cross both the hip and the knee joints, must be extensible. You may have performed a field flexibility test for the hamstrings called the sit-and-reach test. This test is validated against the joint kinematic measurements made by clinicians. If a coach or strength and conditioning advisor measures a lack of flexibility with a field test, he will either help you with this limitation or refer you to medical assistance. Clinicians use joint kinematic measurements as one piece of evidence from many other sources of evidence to diagnose musculoskeletal problems.

Recent research I have conducted with advanced and intermediate players shows successful moderate topspin forehands projected between 1 and 16 degrees. This agrees with the purely mechanical analysis of the physics of ball flight, but the effect of biomechanics was also apparent. Both the advanced and intermediate players tended to have a mean ball trajectory in their successful

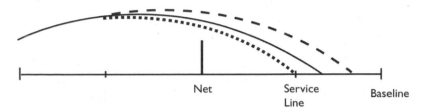

Figure 1.7 *Predicted trajectory for a typical (56 mph) forehand without spin. The same stroke hit with moderate (about 1000 rpm) topspin (. . . . .) and backspin are also illustrated (_ _ _). Adapted with permission from Brody (1987).*

forehands that was closer to one error (in the net or long) than another. Consequently, they tended to make more of one error than another, and their margin for error was not as large as the purely physics-based theory of the flight of the ball (Brody, 1987). Coaches need to apply the information in Chapters 4 and 5 with care because they need to observe the tendencies of each player and integrate that with the windows of optimal projection in tennis. A player who is beginning to make more and more groundstoke errors long should not automatically elicit from the coach a cue to hit closer to the net. The coach needs to observe the pattern in the players racquet path (spin), ball trajectory, and other impact factors before suggesting changes.

SPIN

The Spin Principle states that ball spin can be used to modify ball flight and bounce. The majority of ball spin comes from the bounce on the court, but tennis players hit shots with spin primarily to gain an advantage in ball flight. Topspin groundstrokes are usually used because the spin creates a downward and backward fluid force (known as a lift force or Magnus force) that adds to the effect of gravity and increases the downward curve of the ball (see Integration Box 1.3). This offers obvious tactical advantages such as decreasing the risk of hitting long or keeping the ball low in a passing shot. On the other hand, backspin is often used on an approach shot because the lift force now acts upward and forward and has the desirable effect of decreasing the effect of gravity to create a flat trajectory and lower bounce than topspin strokes (Figure 1.8). An example of a stroke that uses spin to modify ball bounce are drop shots. Drop shots are hit with a higher and slower trajectory and extreme backspin that creates a high (from the trajectory), slow (from both the slow speed and the backspin) bounce.

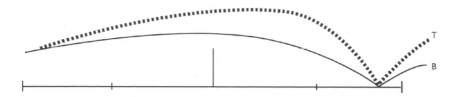

Figure 1.8 *The flat trajectory of a groundstroke hit with backspin is the primary reason balls with backspin do not appear to bounce as high as strokes with topspin (. . . .).*

The relationship between ball spin and stroke margin for error is also a complicated issue. Researchers have measured the drag (backward) and lift forces created by air flow past tennis balls (Goodwill et al., 2004; Mehta and Pallis, 2001). These data must be combined with computer modeling and experimental validation with actual tennis players before players and coaches can know the optimal projection windows for shots with varying (none, small, medium, and large) amounts of spin.

The Spin Principle states that ball spin can be used to modify ball flight and bounce.

Validation data using tennis players are important to examine interactions of variables in realistic conditions. For example, many tennis players believe that increasing topspin increases the margin for error in groundstrokes. Based on the ball flight (Optimal Projection) alone, it is true that this will increase the range of launch angles for which the ball will land in the opposite court. It is not so obvious if this improved probability is greater than the probability of a miss-hit or the ball landing short in the court and decreasing your probability of winning the point. This interaction of factors is difficult to study scientifically (see Integration Box 1.3). The following chapters will give general guidelines for techniques to use to create spin typical of skilled tennis players. The individual player will have to decide how much spin he wants to use on strokes based on his ability, opponent, and situation.

SUMMARY AND MATCH POINTS

Sport biomechanics is the science that strives to understand the motion and causes of motion of humans in sports. Tennis coaches and players should use

Integration Box 1.3

Physics of Ball Spin

Some players can create large amounts of ball spin with their strokes, but this often turns out to be less than the changes in spin that occur when the ball bounces on the court. Cross (2002) notes that typical values of topspin created by the ball bouncing on the court are up to 6,000 revolutions per minute (rpm). Research on elite players using high-speed video cameras have observed topspin groundstrokes and serves with 1,200 to 5,000 rpm of ball rotation (Pallis et al. 1997). Ball spin creates a lift force from the altered airflow over the ball (Figure 1.9). This lift force has a dramatic effect on the trajectory of the ball, which in turn affects the speed and bounce of the ball off the court. A good example is that a ball with backspin will tend to bounce more steeply than a ball

with topspin for the same impact conditions (angle and speed), but backspin approach shots appear to bounce lower than topspin approaches because the lift force in flight creates a flatter trajectory and approach angle to the court. In other words, in actual tennis play an underspin stroke rarely approaches the court at as steep angle as a topspin stroke and so does not bounce as steeply or as high. The exception is a well executed drop shot that would clearly bounce higher than a ball with topspin and a similar speed and trajectory. So determining the best amount of spin to put on a stroke is a complex problem that must be based on initial ball speed/spin, tactical situation, opponent tendencies, and your ability.

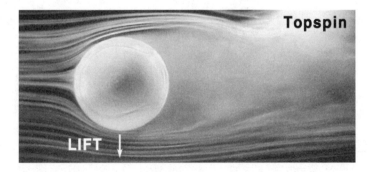

Figure 1.9 Air flow over a tennis ball with topspin in a wind tunnel. The top-spin of the ball deflects the wake upward behind the ball resulting in a downward lift force on the ball. This downward lift force added to the downward effect of gravity creates the steep downward curve late in the trajectory of topspin strokes. (Photo adapted and courtesy of NASA Ames Research Center fluid Mechanics Laboratory and Cislunar Aerospace, Inc.)

sport biomechanics knowledge to help improve stroke and court movement techniques to improve performance or reduce the risk of injury. The consensus of biomechanical research on tennis can be better understood and applied using six general principles of tennis mechanics. The biomechanical principles related to stroke and player movements are force and time, coordination and transfer of energy, balance and inertia, and range of motion. The mechanical principles related to tennis shots are optimal projection and spin.

Match Points

- There is no always right and wrong way to stroke a tennis ball. The principles of biomechanics provide a toolbox of guidelines for making technique decisions that are likely to be more effective and with a lower risk of injury.

- Racquet motion can be created by both greater application of force/torque and applying them over a longer time interval.

- Sequential coordination of many body segments is desirable in tennis because of the relatively small inertia of the arm/racquet and the ability of this coordination to transfer energy through the body to the racquet.

- Balance is the ability to control body motion and players must select technique that is the best compromise between stability and mobility.

- The biomechanics and geometry of tennis means that there are a range of shot angles or windows of success for most strokes.

INJURY PREVENTION IN TENNIS

"Too many people practice their mistakes continuously, and so, become more and more perfect at making errors"—Bobby Riggs

Tennis is a popular sport because players of all abilities can play for a life-time with a relatively low risk of injury. The paradox is that the repetitive motions in tennis can provide for healthful conditioning of the whole body or can accumulate stress on the body that contributes to injury. Bobby Riggs quote could as easily be extended to say that consistent stroking errors could cost you more than points in a match—they could contribute to an injury.

The statistical study of sports injuries in order to try to infer their causative factors is called "epidemiology." Although the mechanism of most injuries is complicated by many contributing factors, this chapter surveys some general patterns in the tennis epidemiology research and focuses on what biomechanical studies show might be important risk reduction strategies. The chapter will conclude with the biomechanical principles related to an important injury-preventing technique common to all tennis strokes—the follow-through. An extensive summary of the treatment and prevention of common tennis injuries is available (Pluim and Safran, 2004), and the USTA also has an excellent white paper on tennis technique and injury (Kibler et al. 2004).

Chapter Two

TENNIS INJURIES

Most tennis players experience very few serious injuries. Injuries to the legs are more common than injuries to the arms or back in skilled tennis players (Kibler and Safran, 2000). Sport injuries are usually classified as acute or overuse.

Acute injuries are sudden onset events like ankle sprains or broken bones, where the structural integrity of a tissue is damaged by a load greater than the mechanical strength of that tissue. An ankle sprain is overstretching of the ligaments around the ankle and is the most common tennis injury.

Overuse injuries appear as gradually developing conditions because even small (apparently noninjurious) loads repeated many times without adequate rest can slowly overcome the recovery process and create an injury. When an athlete falls and fractures his arm, the pain and disability of this acute injury are obvious. An overuse injury, like a stress fracture in the arm, is more difficult to detect.

A stress fracture consists of microscopic breaks in the cortical bone (dense outside layer) that is created by repetitive loading without adequate recovery time. Stress fractures are common in the feet and lower legs of runners, and the only warning sign is a dull pain in the affected bone. Tennis players used to develop stress fractures primarily in the feet and legs, but sports medicine journals have recently (last 5 to 10 years) begun to document stress fractures in the upper extremity of tennis players.

Biomechanical strategies to reduce the risk of stress fractures in the upper extremity include use of a two-handed backhand and strategic adjustments in one's game to roughly equalize forehand and backhand strokes. Playing more matches on clay than hard courts might also reduce the risk of large peak forces on the lower extremities that contribute to stress fractures. Other keys to reducing the risk of stress fractures are adequate calcium intake in your diet and giving your body adequate rest. Very hard matches or practice sessions should be followed by a day off or lighter practice sessions. This cycling of the intensity of training over short and long time intervals is called periodization. Strength and conditioning research has shown that proper periodization is important to maximize the positive effects of training. The programmed rest in these forms of training also likely decreases the risk of overuse injury. Unfortunately, the research on this new form of training in a complex sport like tennis is limited (Kraemer et al. 2000, 2003), so most programs are based on general principles of work to recovery (Baechle and Earle, 2000). Most tennis players should "listen" to their body and qualitatively cycle the intensity of their practice/conditioning with adequate rest and recovery.

This cycling of the intensity of training over short and long time intervals is called periodization. Strength and conditioning research has shown that proper periodization is important to maximize the positive effects of training.

An overuse injury affecting soft tissue common in tennis is "tennis elbow." "Tennis elbow" is a catch-all term for a variety of overuse injuries to the forearm muscle attachments at the elbow. The forearm muscles that flex your wrist (move it in the direction of your palm) all attach to the medial epicondyle (large bony elbow bump inside or next to your body). When these muscles are

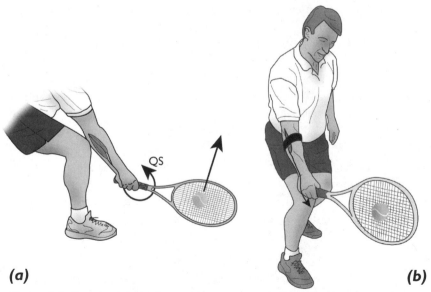

(a)   *(b)*

Figure 2.1 *The shock wave from impact in a one-handed backhand creates a quick stretch (QS) of the forearm extensor muscles that may cause tennis elbow (a), and counter-force braces appear to reduce some of this shock that is transmitted to the painful muscle attachment at the elbow (b).*

overused from serving and forehands, there can be pain on the inside of the elbow. Classic tennis elbow results from overuse of the wrist extensor (forearm muscles moving the hand back) attachment at the lateral epicondyle (large outside bump at the elbow). One-handed backhands are most strongly related to lateral tennis elbow (Figure 2.1a). The shock wave in the racquet from ball impact (see the following section on racquets) stretches the wrist extensor muscles more in players with tennis elbow than pros who have not had tennis elbow (Knudson and Blackwell, 1997).

Overuse (too much physical activity without enough rest for recovery) of muscle-tendon units often results in irritation of the tendon, usually near the muscle-tendon junction. This condition is called lateral epicondylagia (outside of the elbow pain) and is a complex condition with several abnormal physiological mechanisms (Waugh, 2005). Rest and reduction in tennis play often helps resolve this condition, but although there are many physical treatments for tennis elbow, there is not conclusive evidence of success and only limited evidence of the effectiveness of manipulation and exercise (Bisset et al. 2005). Many players receive some relief from the pain with the use of counter-force braces (Figure 2.1b). Counterforce braces appear to dampen shock waves and distribute some muscle forces to other tissues besides the inflamed muscle-tendon junction. Use of braces and over-the-counter anti-inflammatory drugs (NSAIDS) may decrease the symptoms of tennis elbow but should not be used in the place of rest from the strokes that created the condition.

When a player continues to play through pain and does not rest, what might be a inflammatory response (tendonitis) can worsen to degeneration of the tissue (tendinosis). There are a variety of substructures of tendon and pathophysiological causes of tendinopathy (sport injuries to tendon), and sometimes these conditions can develop without obvious symptoms (Maffulli et al. 2003). One of the latest hypotheses being examined as the cause of tendinopathy is stretch stimulating apoptosis, the normal process of programmed cell death (Yuan et al. 2003). Treatment for tendinosis sometimes requires surgery to remove the damaged tissue and rest.

 When a player continues to play through pain and does not rest, what might be a inflammatory response (tendonitis) can worsen to degeneration of the tissue (tendinosis).

Figure 2.2 *Weight training increases the size and strength of muscles and tendons, decreasing their susceptibility of being overloaded. The shoulder abductor and wrist extensor exercise illustrated is recommended to reduce the risk of lateral tennis elbow (Knudson and Blackwell, 1997).*

Strategies hypothesized to prevent tennis elbow include conditioning, equipment, and biomechanical changes. Increasing the strength of the muscle-tendon unit with strength training, naturally increases the tolerance of the tissue to the forces that tend to create injury (Figure 2.2). Decreasing the stiffness of the racquet, increasing racquet mass, and decreasing string tension all decrease the size of the peak force and shock wave transmitted to the hand and arm by ball impact. Using a two-handed backhand, decreasing grip pressure, and decreasing stroke speed/intensity are biomechanical strategies that are effective in reducing the impulsive load transmitted to the body.

While tennis provides a good whole-body workout, there can be a tendency for some players to develop strength and flexibility imbalances from the asymmetric nature of their games, repetition of errors in technique, or individual susceptibility. This tendency became apparent in the mid-twentieth century in many elite tennis players. Many pros that only played tennis and performed no other conditioning exercises developed large-muscled racquet arms and a drooped, over-stretched shoulder (Priest and Nagle, 1976). For example, a player who emphasizes powerful forehands and avoids his one-handed backhand can develop a large dominant arm with stronger chest muscles and over-stretched upper back muscles. Common strength and flexibility imbalances in tennis include: stronger and inflexible shoulder internal rotators, increased trunk extensor strength, and decreased hip internal rotation flexibility (Chandler et al. 1998; Vad et al. 2003). These maladaptations (adverse changes in body tissues and motions) can cause problems at the affected area of the body and in other areas of the body that might also be overused to compensate for the developing problem. Good coaching and conditioning programs can reduce the risk of these overuse injuries.

 Common strength and flexibility imbalances in tennis include: stronger and inflexible shoulder internal rotators, increased trunk extensor strength, and decreased hip internal rotation flexibility.

Fortunately, the last few decades have seen more and more serious tennis players performing conditioning programs (cross-training) in order to improve their performance and maintain healthy strength and flexibility balance in the body. Let's, therefore, turn to issues in tennis-specific and complimentary physical training programs.

WARM-UP AND CONDITIONING

The best injury preventative strategies are likely to be proper warm-up and conditioning for tennis. A proper warm-up ensures that the body tissues will be able to withstand the greatest forces before they are damaged. Proper supplemental conditioning provides the body with greater strength, endurance, flexibility, and other physical capacities to withstand the rigors of tennis play. Both these strategies have undergone considerable change in recent years for tennis players.

Warm-up activities for all sports used to include stretching exercises. Recent research has shown that this belief (it was not based on experimental data) is incorrect, so warm-up should not normally include static stretching (Knudson et al. 2000). Stretching is beneficial for maintaining range of motion, but this should be scheduled during the cool-down from training or match play (Knudson, 2003b).

Warm-up should consist of general whole-body movements that gradually increase in intensity, focusing extra movement for joints and muscles to be used in practice or competition. General warm-up consists of whole-body movements up to 40 to 60 percent of maximum aerobic capacity for 5 to 10 minutes. Tennis players might do 5 minutes of light jogging followed by USTA dynamic warm-up exercises (USTA, 2004) or the traditional five-minute warm-up of groundstrokes and serves prior to a match.

Warm-up activities for all sports used to include stretching exercises. Recent research has shown that this belief is incorrect, so warm-up should not normally include static stretching.

Warm-up increases the blood flow and temperature of muscles. Increasing tissue temperature increases the mechanical strength—the force/energy that can be absorbed by the tissue before it is damaged. Normal movements and muscle contractions decrease muscle passive tension and increase range of motion as much or more than passive stretching (Knudson, in press).

Conditioning to reduce risk of injury in tennis includes a variety of exercise programs. Traditional weight training, calisthenics, stretching/yoga, tennis drills, running, and other sports have all been used to improve several fitness variables for tennis players. Recent emphasis has been placed on functional testing and conditioning exercises (Figure 2.3a) and Swiss ball exercises (Figure 2.3b) that require greater muscle activation to stabilize the body compared to similar exercises on stable, firm surfaces. This trend of greater use of multi-joint exercises, lower resistances, higher speeds, and incorporating greater balance requirements has improved the specificity of tennis conditioning.

Specificity of training is a well-known principle of conditioning that maintains that the characteristics of the exercises (body position, range of motion, and speed) should match the movement of interest. For example, conditioning

This trend of greater use of multi-joint exercises, lower resistances, higher speeds, and incorporating greater balance requirements has improved the specificity of tennis conditioning.

research from several decades ago demonstrated that the common notion of muscular strength really is manifested in three different performance domains, static (little motion-high-force/resistance), dynamic (motion and resistance), and explosive (high motion-low resistance). Most tennis movements fall in the latter two categories, so most tennis conditioning exercises should emphasize moderate loads, quick movement, and tennis-like movements. Readers interested in conditioning programs designed to be tennis-specific (improve performance and combat tennis-specific asymmetries) are referred to the books by Chu (1995), Roetert and Ellenbecker (2002), and Reid et al. (2003).

Most tennis players would benefit from a general, supplementary conditioning program based on these resources. Serious tournament players would be wise to consult a certified strength and conditioning specialist (CSCS certification given by the National Strength and Conditioning Association [NSCA]) who can customize all aspects of a conditioning program based on the

Figure 2.3 *Functional tests and exercises do not isolate specific joints or artificially stabilize the body like exercise machines (a), and exercises on unstable surfaces like a Swiss ball are currently popular because they tend to use greater muscle activation to help stabilize the body.*

Most tennis conditioning exercises should emphasize moderate loads, quick movement, and tennis-like movements.

Advantage Box 2.1: Biomechanics of Stretching

It is safe to say that biomechanical and medical research beginning in the 1990s began to change the common beliefs about stretching. Basic research with animal and human muscles showed that static stretching exercises created weakening of the muscle much like other forms of training. Tissues that are stressed by exercise normally require 24 to 48 hours of rest to recover and improve to these new demands placed on them. Studies of animal and human muscles also consistently reported that repeated stretching decreases passive resistance early in the range of motion (this stress relaxation is easily felt by people), but did not change the stiffness of the tissue as it reaches the limits of the typical range of motion. In other words, stretching will tend to make you weaker and the muscle will not be more compliant (be able to stretch significantly further with lower force in the tissue before injury).

These data combined with the surprising results of prospective studies of troops in military basic training showing no injury protective benefit of stretching prior to exercise is beginning to change the previous dogma of stretching in the warm-up. There were never any studies that supported the logic of this old belief, but now we know that warm-up is the most important injury reducing strategy prior to vigorous activity. Tennis players should stretch after matches and strive to maintain normal levels of flexibility. There is no proven benefit of creating greater than normal flexibility. In fact, the stability-mobility paradox and some epidemiology data from running sports suggests that too much flexibility may also increase injury risk just like very low flexibility can.

player's individual needs. Good conditioning increases the mechanical strength of key tissues (muscle, tendons, ligaments, bones) and will likely decrease the risk of injury during tennis play.

TECHNIQUE

The techniques used in tennis naturally affect which body tissues are loaded and may be exposed to risk of injury. This book touches on this topic and provides detailed explanations of tennis techniques and what biomechanical research on these techniques tells us about how to decrease the risk of injury.

Integration Box 2.1
Perfect or Optimal Technique

Athletes are often searching for the perfect or optimal technique. Unfortunately, differences in individuals in a dynamic sport like tennis mean that there is no perfect technique for particular strokes (Groppel, 1992). There is also no perfect technique that ensures a player won't be injured. Some people have anatomical or physiological traits that makes them susceptible to a particular injury. You could step on a ball walking onto a tennis court and sprain your ankle! Remember that Chapter 1 noted that the principles of biomechanics suggest that certain patterns of movement best suit the human body and a particular task. It is best that players and coaches strive to identify and focus on principle-based commonalities of tennis technique rather than searching for a perfect technique. A player might find that even their favorite stroke that seems to be naturally self-optimized, gradually changes over the years. Ask an experienced player what aging has done to his or her strokes.

Specific tennis technique examples will be discussed in the following chapters, but this section will give a simple example of how biomechanics can be used to prescribe a technique adjustment that might decrease the risk of injury in the serve.

Advanced players often learn to hit a twist serve. A twist serve produces a great deal of topspin on the ball by an exaggerated upward brushing of the ball by the racquet strings. A right-handed player would traditionally toss the ball slightly more overhead and arch his back more in preparation to get greater upward racquet motion than a typical flat or slice (ball sidespin) serve. Biomechanical studies of the lower back have shown, however, that this arching (low back hyperextension) dramatically increases pressure and stress in the disks and small facet joints in the spine. The disks and long ligaments of the spine are weaker in the back than in the front. This combined with the research on the benefits of greater knee bend and extension in the serve provides an argument for changing the classic twist serve technique. Most players should strive to create the upward and to the right (for a right-hander) racquet motion in a twist serve with different preparatory motions (Figure 2.4). Players hitting twist serves should strive to emphasize greater knee bend with less low back hyperextension. A strong leg drive and upward racquet motion can then create the racquet motion without potentially dangerous localized loading in the lower back.

Figure 2.4 *The safest preparatory motions to create the up and to the right racquet motion for a twist serve (right-handed player) emphasize knee bend rather than arching the back.*

EQUIPMENT

The equipment tennis players select also has an influence on the risk of injury. Everything from shoes, clothing, grips, racquets, and strings all potentially contribute to a player's risk of injury during tennis play. This section cannot review all of these factors, much less their interaction, but it will summarize some major trends for racquets, strings, balls, and shoes. Racquets and shoes interact with the human body and, therefore, are topics where biomechanical studies have been conducted. People interested in more information on how technology and equipment affect tennis play should read *The Physics and Technology of Tennis* by Brody, Cross and Lindsey (2002) or *Technical Tennis* by Cross and Lindsey (2005).

RACQUETS AND STRINGS

Tennis players often have a love affair with the sport and with a particular racquet. Maybe it's your current frame, or maybe it was an old favorite that is no longer available. Tennis is also a sport where the "feel" of a racquet during the swing or at impact with the ball is held in high esteem. While this aesthetic dimension of the game is important, it may not be as important as tennis folklore suggests. This section outlines what we know about the biomechanics of tennis racquets and highlights a few ways to customize your racquet's performance. Much more detail on this topic is provided by Brody, Cross, and Lindsey (2002).

One persistent myth is that grip strength can be used to increase the speed of the ball off the racquet. This belief is likely based on decades of tennis coaching that emphasized use of firm grip and the common experience of miss-hitting a volley or stroke using a weak grip, usually with disastrous results. The problem with this perception is that the slow and errant ball rebound was caused by a low racquet speed and off-center impact location on the strings. The exaggerated recoil of the racquet on a miss-hit is symptomatic and occurs long after the ball has rebounded from the strings (usually in 4 to 5 milliseconds).

In tennis the "feel" of a racquet during the swing or at impact with the ball is held in high esteem. While this aesthetic dimension of the game is important, it may not be as important as tennis folklore suggests.

Hand forces at the grip of a tennis racquet have no significant effect on the speed or accuracy of ball rebound during impact, so the real-world impact response of tennis racquets is as if the racquet were not being held (Knudson 1997; Knudson and Elliott, 2004). In other words, the racquet's reponse is primarily mechnical (based on mechanical properties of the frame, strings, and the ball), not biomechanical (influence by the player's hand). The grip forces are only influential in that they help to create racquet speed, intercept the ball, and control the racquet after impact. When tennis players say they admire another player's great "feel," they are likely admiring his pre-impact racquet control that manifests itself in precisely adjusted ball speed and spin off the racquet.

Hand forces at the grip of a tennis racquet have no significant effect on the speed or accuracy of ball rebound during impact.

Figure 2.5 illustrates very high-speed (1,800 frames per second) images of an experimental tennis impact, the equivalent of a two-handed reflex volley. Note how much the player's racquet, hands, and forearms recoil after the ball has already rebounded, even with a two-handed grip! Very high-speed images of groundstrokes often show a similar pattern of a violent shock wave slowing the racquet and jolting the player's hand and arm. In groundstrokes, the arm recoil can be even larger than in Figure 2.5 because there is often only one arm and the closing speed between the racquet and ball is larger. This very short duration but large force loading is invisible to the naked eye or normal video replay (30 frames per second).

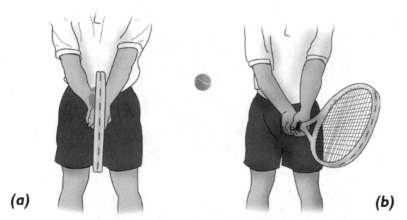

(a) **(b)**

Figure 2.5 *The recoil of a tennis player's hand and arm from the shock wave of a 52 mph impact are illustrated for a static impact simulating a two-handed volley. Images were drawn from high-speed (1800 pictures per second) film. , the first image (a) is near maximum compression of the ball (about 3 milliseconds after string contact) and the second image (b) is 17 ms after initial ball-string contact. Note the large recoil (8 inch) and twisting of the racquet from the force of impact.*

Shock or Vibration?

Portions of this chapter have discussed the prevention of the overuse injury called tennis elbow. The technique or equipment modifications a tennis player selects should be related to minimizing the mechanical origin of the condition. The two variables that have been examined are the initial shock wave and frame vibrations created by ball impact. Several observations from the many studies on this topic follow:

1. Most of the energy (about 63%) of the deformation of the racquet after impact resides in the initial shock wave with a smaller percentage in racquet vibration (Knudson, 2004).

2. Hand forces easily damp out frame vibrations in the 40 to 50 ms after impact (Figure 2.6).

3. Tennis elbow is most likely a result of eccentric stretching (activated muscles being forcibly stretched) of forearm muscles by the initial shock wave of impact rather than frame vibration (Knudson, 2004).

4. String vibration dampers reduce the high-pitched "ping" of string vibration. String vibrations have very little energy, and research has shown that string dampers have no effect on the shock or vibration of the frame that load the player's hand and arm (Li et al. 2004; Stoede et al. 1999).

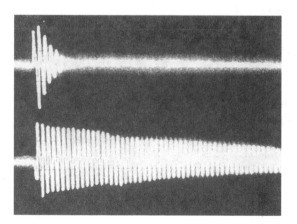

Figure 2.6 *Frame vibrations are quickly damped out by hand forces compared to a freely vibrating racquet. (Used with permission from Brody, Cross, and Lindsey [2002].)*

Decreasing string tension creates a slightly longer ball impact that reduces the peak force transmitted to the frame and arm.

A tennis player with tennis elbow or who is trying to reduce his risk of tennis elbow can alter several racquet variables to help reduce the shock wave of impact. These variables are string tension and frame design (stiffness, mass, and head size). Adjusting these variables is the application of the Force and Time Principle. Selecting these variables to spread the shock wave over a greater time decreases the peak force transmitted to the arm. Smaller forces and shocks mean less stress and stretching of your arm muscles.

Decreasing string tension creates a slightly longer ball impact that reduces the peak force transmitted to the frame and arm. More flexible racquets also serve to dampen the shock wave transmitted to the arm. Since the mass of the racquet is the inertia that must be accelerated by the impact forces, increasing racquet mass (especially in the head) will help reduce impact shock. Larger head frames also have advantages in reducing the shock transmitted to the body. The major advantage is greater resistance to twisting from off-center impacts. See Brody, Cross, and Lindsey (2002) on how to use lead tape to modify racquet mass and resistance to rotation about the long axis of the racquet.

BALLS

There are several kinds of balls legal for tennis play. Most tennis balls are manufactured with internal pressures to combine with the material properties of the rubber core and felt to meet the rebound specifications of the rules of tennis. Many players can feel and hear subtle differences when playing with different tennis balls. Many players report that hitting pressureless (made with stiffer rubber to create the desired bounce) or the larger type 3 tennis balls feel harder than regular tennis balls. Research directly comparing the type 3 ball to regular tennis balls, however, has shown that some individuals might adjust their strokes and experience a larger shock with this ball, this effect is very small and is not present for most players, so there is likely no significant difference in the risk of injury between tennis balls (Andrew et al. 2003; Blackwell and Knudson, 2002; Knudson and Blackwell, 2001). There is more likely a greater risk of loading and injury if players play matches on windy days or try to hit their strokes harder.

The material properties of tennis balls have much less to do with the mechanics of tennis impacts than other (player, racquet, impact location, ball speed) factors. Just as the arm and racquet experience a shock wave and post-impact vibrations, so does the ball. Figure 2.5 shows the considerable flattening of the ball during impact, but Figure 2.7 shows the post-impact ball vibrations following a flat serve. On returning to normal shape following impact the ball still vibrates.

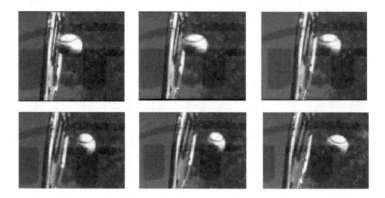

Figure 2.7 *Ultra-high speed (6,000 frames per second) video images of the vibration of a tennis ball following impact in a flat serve. The ball wobbles or vibrates between the six images. (Images courtesy of the International Tennis Federation.)*

Shoes

Tennis shoes, like all athletic shoes, must be designed with two opposing performance demands—shock absorption and control/protection of the foot. The softer the midsole (layer between the external surface and the lining material in the shoe) material in the shoe, the better its shock absorption capability. Unfortunately, this allows more motion of the foot than a harder midsole material. A tennis player moving laterally with worn-out, very soft, or poorly fitting shoes with little support could increase the risk of an ankle sprain (Figure 2.8). A sprain is damaged ligaments at a joint. If a shoe is constructed with less cushioning in the midsole, there will be less motion allowed, but greater loading of the body. This greater pounding of the joints poses a different risk of injury. Tennis players running and cutting on a tennis court typically experiences peak vertical ground reaction forces under a foot between 2.0 and 2.6 times their body weight. Landing from a jump or lunge can increase the peak force on a foot up to 4 to 6 bodyweights.

Biomechanical studies have been conducted on the effectiveness of various tennis shoes in controlling foot motion and interacting with court surfaces. Injury rates are higher on hard court surfaces compared to soft court surfaces

> **It appears that there is no one best tennis shoe and that each player will have biomechanical characteristics that match some shoes better than others.**

(Nigg and Segesser, 1988), but shoe characteristics appear to have a greater influence on foot loading than court surface (Dixon and Stiles, 2003). Making the picture even more complicated, individual players have unique responses to tennis shoes of similar cushioning properties (Hreljac, 1998; Nigg, Luthi, and Bahlsen, 1989). It appears that there is no one best tennis shoe and that each player will have biomechanical characteristics that match some shoes better than others. Elite athletes with endorsement contracts with shoes bearing

Figure 2.8 *Changing directions laterally or catching the edge of your shoe are common causes of ankle sprains in tennis players.*

their name often have customized models made for them, with the shoes in the stores having at most a cosmetic resemblance to the shoes the athlete wears.

So how should a player select tennis shoes to reduce his risk of injury? It is clear from the research that shoes have been designed with a wide range of friction characteristics to match the range of court surfaces in tennis. Once a player selects shoes designed for the court he usually plays on, he should consider his style of play, foot type, and comfort to help him select tennis shoes.

Lower-level recreational players tend to load different parts of the foot more than advanced or competitive players (Nigg, Luthi, and Bahlsen, 1989). An advanced player who rushes the net often should look for shoes with adequate cushioning in the forefoot and toe protection. A baseliner who does much more lateral movement would not need to emphasize these features but would benefit from a shoe with a solid heel counter and higher shaft (mid/high-top). Higher top shoes help reduce the risk and severity of ankle spains (Stussi, Stacoff, and Tiegermann, 1989). High-top shoes and ankle braces are effective in reducing the risk of ankle injury by increasing ankle positioning feedback and providing some mechanical support. The negatives for high-top shoes or ankle braces is that there may be some small decreases in performance from the restriction of ankle motion, and the support cannot totally prevent an ankle sprain.

 A net rusher should look for shoes with adequate cushioning in the forefoot and toe protection. A baseliner who does much more lateral movement would benefit from a shoe with a solid heel counter and higher shaft.

A player's foot type provides some general guidance on what amount of cushioning might be best in a shoe. Feet fall on a continuum between flat-feet (pronated) and high-arched feet (supinated). A person with flat-feet has little shock absorbing ability within his feet, while a high-arched foot can flatten out, slowed by stretching the ligaments and muscles in the foot. Players with high-arched feet might select softer midsole materials because foot motion is not a problem, while players with flat feet might select firmer shoes with arch support. These are general guidelines, and the most important indicator of shoe cushioning and support may be comfort.

Since individuals respond to shoes differently and the interaction of shoes and court surfaces varies, it is important for players to let comfort be their guide. Unfortunately, what feels comfortable in the store is not always going to agree with the true idea of comfort. True assessments of comfort are based on how your feet and body feel during and after normal play. Sensations that might be related to a shoe with too much cushioning would be pain outside joints and too much foot motion in the shoe during cutting. Sensations that might be related to shoes with too little cushioning would be sore feet and pain in the ankle joint.

One factor that should be considered to override comfort considerations is shoe wear—if a players' shoes have been worn out in key areas or have been worn for an extended period of time. Research on athletic shoes has shown that the cushioning properties decrease with use. Significant reductions in cushioning, increases in foot pressure, and damage to cells of the foam can occur in as little as 500 miles of running. Tennis players should regularly replace their shoes before they feel discomfort if they have been playing with the shoes for a long time. Players may need to consult with a podiatrist to help them with customizing their shoes/insoles weighing the comfort, wear, anatomical, and motion factors.

FOLLOW-THROUGH

All tennis strokes have a follow-through phase where the kinetic (motion) energy of the racquet and body after impact is dissipated by the body. This is a very important injury prevention strategy because the racquet often can retain over 90 percent of its kinetic energy after impact in tennis strokes. The biomechanical principles supporting this are Force and Time and Range of Motion. Increasing the range of motion and time used in the body motions of a follow-through decrease the peak loads of negative acceleration acting on the body tissues.

When muscles act as brakes slowing the motion of a body segment, they are elongated or stretched while being stimulated. This called an eccentric muscle action and it results in the creation of large forces focused in smaller numbers of muscle fibers. While the body is used to doing this, it is best to decrease the speed of the stretch, thereby decreasing the forces in the muscle.

It would be rare for a tennis player to have too long a follow-through, so it is best to be cautious and use long, complete follow-throughs in strokes. Players can focus on stroking through the impact point, elongating the follow-though toward the target, and then gradually slowing the arm and racquet down. Many times the racquet paths are not as aligned with the target because of the ball trajectory or creating ball spin. In these cases the player should still strive to stroke thorough the ball and gradually slow the racquet as it arcs around the body.

 Increasing the range of motion and time used in the body motions of a follow-through decrease the peak loads of negative acceleration acting on the body tissues.

SUMMARY AND MATCH POINTS

Tennis players enjoy their sport with a relatively low risk of injury. Injuries are classified as acute or overuse. An ankle sprain is a common acute injury in tennis, while tennis elbow is a common overuse injury. Biomechanics helps players reduce their risk of injury by documenting the warm-up and conditioning exercises that are most effective, as well as the equipment and stroke techniques that might have the lowest risk of injury. Elongated follow-throughs in tennis strokes are important to reducing the peak forces on the musculoskeletal system. Peak forces and the stress they create in tissues are the likely causes of injuries in tennis.

Match Points

- Tennis injuries typically have multiple causative factors, but risks can be minimized by modifications in technique, equipment, and conditioning.

- Always warm-up prior to tennis play/practice with progressively increasing whole-body and tennis-specific movements.

- Stretching should not normally be part of the warm-up, but players should stretch after play/practice.

- Conditioning for tennis should be sport-specific (functional movements, moderate resistance, and fast speeds), programmed based on periodization, and target individual problem area or tennis-specific strength/flexibility imbalances.

- Decease the risk of tennis elbow by:
  - -Technique: Slower strokes and a relaxed grip
  - -Equipment: Decrease racquet stiffness and string tension, increase racquet head and mass
  - -Conditioning: Strengthen forearm, arm, and shoulder muscles

- Twist or topspin serves should be created primarily through vigorous knee bend and extension, rather than arching the back.

- A long follow-through is an important injury-prevention strategy in most all tennis strokes.

Chapter Three

BIOMECHANICS OF THE SERVE

"Cut down on your power if your first serve is not going in
at least 70 percent of the time."
—Richard "Pancho" Gonzalez

The serve is the most important stroke in tennis. Powerful servers such as Pancho Gonzales and Pete Sampras have shown how a great serve can dominate the game at the elite level. The serve is also the stroke with the most biomechanical studies on which to draw conclusions. The biomechanical principles and research studies paint a pretty clear general picture on the best techniques to use in the various tennis serves and that some common serve wisdom might be in error.

Traditionally, serves were classified as first or second serves, with first serves being higher-speed (flat) and second serves being slower with greater spin (slice). This terminology is problematic for a couple reasons. First, all serves are hit with spin, so a serve hit will no spin is not possible, and a "flat" serve is a misnomer. A flat serve is just a serve hit to maximize ball speed and, therefore, has minimal spin. Tennis players should think about all serves as having a mix of ball speed and spin that they select based on the match conditions. This complication also affects the biomechanical research on the serve because players hit serves with a mix of spins in competition or in experimental settings. Second, the increased power and accuracy of modern racquets has begun to change this traditional serving strategy. Examination of match statistics has shown that some players may benefit from faster first and second serves, and the common rule of thumb of making 70 percent of first serves might not be the best strategy for all players.

Biomechanically, all serves use the same basic overarm striking pattern. This pattern of motion has many similarities to other sport skills like baseball pitching and the badminton clear. There are, of course, unique adjustments to the basic overarm throwing/striking pattern that are related to the rules of tennis. Superimposed on this serving movement are three basic serving techniques that represent a mix of ball topspin and sidespin: the flat, slice, and twist serves. To create these serves there are subtle adjustments in arm and racquet motion through impact with the ball. There is a strategic advantage to be able to create distinctly different combinations of speed, spin, and placement of serves without major adjustments in technique that can be observed by the opponent receiving serve.

 Some players may benefit from faster first and second serves, and the common rule of thumb of making 70 percent of first serves might not be the best strategy for all players.

Following a short review of the biomechanical significance of the grip in the serve, the biomechanical principles related to the general pattern of the serve will be discussed for the "flat" serve. The rest of the chapter will discuss the principles and research about the slice and twist serves.

GRIP

Advanced tennis players almost always use a continental or backhand grip to serve. This is critical because the eastern forehand grip many beginners learn to serve with, limits wrist motion and can lead to suboptimal racquet paths through impact. A player who has always served with an eastern forehand grip cannot easily add wrist and forearm motion to the throwing action of the arm. This poor application of segment coordination and transfer of energy to the racquet results in lower racquet head speed at impact and, consequently, slower ball speed.

The other problem that tends to develop with an eastern forehand grip is an exaggerated sideward (to the right for a right-handed server) racquet path across the back of the ball to create spin of the serve. The racquet for a right-hander naturally tends to move to the right because of the trunk rotation and arm action (Plagenhoef, 1970). Exaggeration of this racquet path decreases the ball speed on the serve and contributes to the nightmare the player experiences when he tries to change to a continental grip on the serve (see Integration Box 3.1). It turns out that the wrong grip also tends to create the sub-optimal racquet path through impact that affects the optimal projection of the ball. Slower ball speeds do not allow for faster and lower ball trajectories into the service box. Many tennis pros might remember teaching some begnners who actually made early serves with backspin and a soft, upward trajectory. These players limit their wrist motion and body extension at impact so the ball speed is very slow and the ball must travel quite high to reach the service box.

Integration Box 3.1

Continental Grip and the Serve

Many intermediates have a difficult transition from an eastern to a continental grip on the serve. These players learn a sideward racquet path with minimal wrist motion by using the eastern grip on their serve. Switching to the continental they get a slow serve with the ball going to the left (right-handed player) because of a disastous combination of minimal wrist action, the racquet face angled to the left, and their old left to right racquet path through impact. A good slice serve requires a vigorous, driving the racquet through the ball with a slightly angled racquet face. A more glancing racquet path can be developed for greater spin, but this this requires practice and a very fast racquet speed.

The discussion of serve biomechanics that follow assume the player is using a continental or backhand grip. This grip allows for free wrist and forearm action and allows for more effective and wider variety of racquet paths to create speed and spin on the ball. A player serving with a continental grip can swing the racquet more through the ball toward the target allowing the angled racquet face to create spin (Figure 3.1a), while an indirect racquet path with an eastern grip (assuming you could even create the same racquet speed) creates less ball speed (Figure 3.1b). The racquet path at the instant of impact is the racquet velocity. Velocities (vector quantities like force) are illustrated as arrows with the length of the arrow representing size and the tip indicating direction. The size of two horizontal components (parts) of the racquet motion are illustrated. The lateral component contributes to ball spin while the down-the-court component contributes to ball speed. Note how an indirect path of the racquet (3.1b) decreases the down-the-court or ball speed component of the stroke.

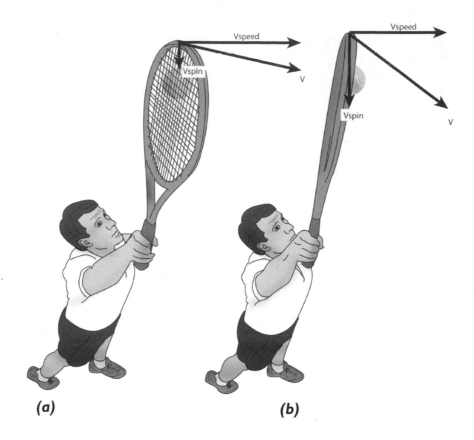

(a)   **(b)**

Figure 3.1 *Top view of typical racquet velocities at impact in an advanced serve with a continental grip (a) and a beginner serve with an eastern grip assuming the same racquet speed (b). The advanced serve with a continental grip is more aligned with the target, creating sidespin and greater ball speed, while a more oblique racquet path creates less ball speed. The right angle components (parts) of each racquet velocity (V) show the compromise between down-the-court (Vspeed) and lateral (Vspin) effects on the ball.*

Another critical concept about the service grip is that the grip pressure needs only to be enough to control the racquet. Excessive grip pressure comes primarily from coactivation of the flexor and extensor muscles of the forearm. This tension on both sides of the wrist joint stiffens the joint and tends to restrict motion at the wrist. This is clearly counterproductive in the serve, so

Advanced tennis players almost always use a continental or backhand grip to serve.

players should strive to keep their grip and whole arm relaxed as they serve. We will see in the next two chapters that the old teaching point of a "firm" grip in groundstrokes is usually counterproductive to high-speed shots also.

The effect of grip and grip pressure on the serve is an example where the biomechanics of the arm and racquet must be integrated with the physics of ball flight to determine the range of optimal projection angles for different serves. The adjustment of the racquet path to create different spin serves is discussed in the sections on the slice and twist serve. We will also see in other strokes that, for a given racquet speed, the selected racquet path represents a compromise between the ball speed and spin that can be created.

"FLAT" SERVE

The flat or power serve in tennis is the serve with the most ball speed, but is not hit without ball spin. Even though the racquet face may be aligned and moving toward the target more than on other serves, the upward and sideward motions of the body and racquet create some topspin and sidespin on the ball (Elliott, 1983). Since this serve represents the end of the continuum of minimizing ball spin and maximizing speed, the biomechanical principles related to the flat serve are primarily related to creating fast and accurate projection of the ball. This analysis of the biomechanics of the flat serve will also summarize the key technique elements in common of all tennis serves.

Footwork: Using Force and Time

Like most strokes, much of the force used to create the stroke originates with the leg drive against the ground. This is the Force and Time Principle at work in the footwork of the serve. The footwork? Don't the rules of tennis require a player to serve from essentially a stationary position behind the baseline? Yes, but careful observers have noted that tennis players do vigorously use their legs, a weight shift, and two distinct footwork techniques (Figure 3.2). These techniques have been called the foot-up (pinpoint) or foot-back (platform) techniques (Elliott and Wood, 1983; Groppel, 1992). Which technique you use does affect the direction and size of the forces you can create to hit your serve.

(a)   **(b)**

Figure 3.2 *(a) The foot-up (pinpoint) and (b) foot-back (platform) techniques of the tennis serve differ near the completion of the preparation phase.*

During the toss and racquet preparation phase of the serve, the foot-up technique moves the rear foot up next to the front foot. This is easily accomplished because the player is bending the knees in a countermovement prior to the vigorous upward hitting action of the forward swing phase. The foot-back technique keeps the rear foot back from the forward foot during the toss and racquet preparations. Studies of these techniques show that the foot-up technique favors generation of vertical ground reaction forces that are effective in creating racquet speed and ball topspin. The wider stance of the foot-back technique creates greater horizontal ground reaction forces that might help serve-and-volley players be quicker into the court following the serve (Figure 3.3).

 **Tennis players use their legs, a weight shift, and two distinct footwork techniques—the foot-up (pinpoint) or foot-back (platform) techniques. Which one you use affects the direction and size of the forces you can create to hit your serve.**

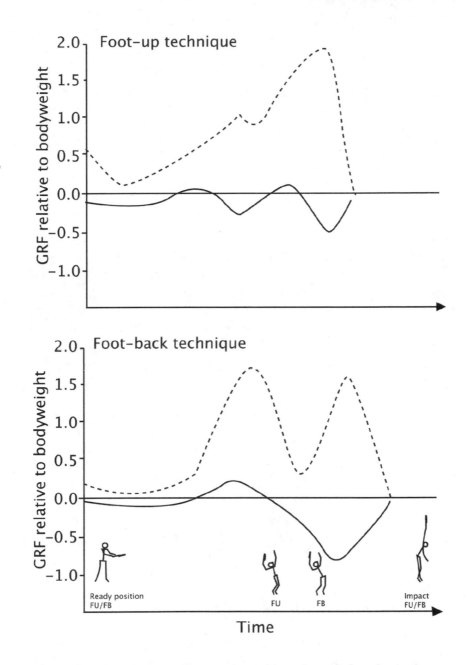

Figure 3.3 *Ground reaction forces measured by a force platform for the foot-up and foot back serve techniques. The foot-up technique favors greater vertical thrust, while the foot-back technique favors the creation of greater forward forces from the ground. (Reproduced with permission from Elliott [1988]).*

Both footwork techniques are effective with elite tennis players pushing so hard off the ground that contact with the ball is made with the player's feet off the ground and usually over the court. It is important to realize that this leg drive is timed and controlled so that energy is transferred up the body and the feet don't leave the ground early in the serve. The strokes' forward motion is initiated while the feet are still on the ground so that the arm and body has a virtually unlimited inertia base to push off from. Leaving the ground before the initiation of the swing would be counterproductive, since the forward swing could then only be generated by pushing off the player's own body mass. We will return to this transfer of energy later in this section after discussing the controlled nature of this stroke.

Optimizing Speed and Accuracy: Balance and Inertia at Work

The tennis serve can only be effectively high-speed if the player has enough control to place the ball in the service box. There is a large body of research in biomechanics and other sport sciences on these speed-accuracy activities, showing there is a speed-accuracy trade-off. That is, the accuracy requirements of a skill like the tennis serve or a golf swing impose limitations on how the striking implement speed is created. This strong influence of control of the racquet means that tennis players need to be concerned with the principle of balance and Inertia in the serve.

A player who tends to have a high-speed but inconsistent toss and service motion should consider technique changes that improve control of stability over the great motion and vigor that seems natural to them. This kind of player might strive to use a foot-back technique and focus on a more "relaxed" effort than straining to achieve a maximum and/or train to improve balance. Ironically, sometimes it is the straining to achieve maximum effort in high-speed skills like the serve that interferes with good balance and coordination and actually decreases performance. Remember, because the serve is a linked chain of sequential movements, any small error along the way can be magnified as its effect is passed from one segment to the next, each compensating for the "correction" of the previous one. A classic example is a player trying so hard for a big (fast) first serve that he grips too firmly and actually restricts

Because the serve is a linked chain of sequential movements, any small error along the way can be magnified as its effect is passed from one segment to the next, each compensating for the "correction" of the previous one.

wrist motion and the transfer of energy from the arm to the racquet, decreasing serve speed.

Other players might naturally have a service technique with constrained motion that provides consistency and control, but lacks the power to create high racquet speeds. A player with this tendency might move toward a foot-up technique that would increase the complexity and narrow the base of support. These changes favor motion over stability, increasing the balance demands of the skill. If the player has the balance to consistently execute this movement, the potential increases in upward range of motion and vertical transfer of energy might result in better (higher racquet speed) performance over time.

It is important to note that these two scenarios are common, but not always consistent for all players. Striking the right mix of effort/balance in the serves is like the speed/accuracy tradeoff in many sports. Individuals will have various capabilities that affect how well they control the inertia of their body or external objects like a tennis racquet. It is possible that an injury or a new racquet might affect the service technique that would be best for a player.

Two other serve elements are strongly affected by the principle of balance and inertia: the toss and the backswing. Research has again shown that players have been successful with a variety of tosses and racquet backswings. The best toss or backswing for a particular player may depend on his balance, ability, temperament, and strategic factors.

The toss of the serve must positioned to allow for contact with the ball with the body and racquet nearly fully extended vertically and timed to the whole service motion. The rules allow for any contact point before the ball bounces, but high contact points provide the most aggressive angles into the service box. There has been debate on the exact height and placement of the toss relative to the server's body. Research has shown that players hit the ball on the way up, near the peak of the toss, and on the way down. The advantages of the first two are a quick service delivery that is less susceptible to the wind. Higher tosses that allow the ball to drop prior to racquet contact have greater energy and contribute to greater topspin on the serve. Timing of each of these tosses has virtually the same margin for error, so what height of the toss is best depends on the environmental conditions and the timing of the player's serve.

Balance and accuracy can be adversely affected by the ball toss if there are side-to-side or forward-backward errors in the toss. In general, research has shown that tosses in flat and slice serves are made so the ball is contacted slightly forward of the baseline and to right of the hitting shoulder (right handed player). Twist serves are often hit off tosses closer to directly overhead. There is variation in the location of the toss across players and within-players, but the goal should always be to minimize this variation in the toss to increase accuracy and the deception in your serve. Many players have a tendency to toss the ball too far to their left (right-handed server) because of the rotation of the joints of the tossing arm are in that direction. Inconsistency in toss placement affects balance because the player must move his body to accommodate the errant toss. A right-hander leaning backward and bending to the left to chase a bad toss places great strain on the lower back to adjust the swing to impact the ball. Combinations of sideward bending and twistng are some of the most dangerous motions for the lower back.

 Players have been successful with a variety of tosses and racquet backswings. The best toss or backswing for a particular player may depend on his balance, ability, temperament, and strategic factors.

While the tossing arm is in motion, the racquet arm and body are also making preparatory actions for the serve. The racquet arm has traditionally been dropped and lifted in synchrony with the tossing arm. This large looping backswing appears to aid in synchronization of the arm and body action and set-up a more vigorous stretch of the arm muscles that accelerate the racquet. Interestingly, there is initial data that this technique is not superior to an abbreviated backswing (Elliott, Fleisig, Nicholls, & Escamilla, 2003). This study of Olympic competitors showed that players using an abbreviated backswing in the serve had similar ball speeds and peak loads (torques) in the major joints of the serving arm. Another study of collegiate players has supported this observaton of similar performance and shoulder loading between these two serve styles (Shapiro et al. submitted).

Maximizing Racquet Speed:
Coordination and Transfer of Energy Are Key
Almost every tennis player would love to increase the speed of his serve. The most important factor in creating high-speed shots is maximizing racquet head speed at impact through proper Coordination and Transfer of Energy. Fortunately, there is a large body of research on the tennis serve and high-

speed and accuracy overarm movements like the serve. These bodies of litera-ture agree on some general answers as to what the best coordination would be for a high-speed tennis (flat) serve.

A high-speed, accurate movement performed with a small inertia implement such as a tennis racquet tends to use a sequential coordination pattern. This means that many body segments are used in a sequence from large to small. Large segments far from the racquet initiate the movement followed by a care-fully timed sequence moving to the smaller segments (Figure 3.4). In theory this is logical because the lower extremity and trunk have the largest segments with the largest, most powerful muscle groups. As mechanical energy is chan-neled to the smaller segments, their smaller muscles can assist in the transfer and add mechanical energy to speed up the distal segments. The smaller mass-es and moments of inertia (angular inertia or resistance to rotation) of the smaller segments also allow for the rapid acceleration of these segments.

Figure 3.4 *The sequential coordination of a linked segment system transfers energy from the larger to the smaller segments in a sequence. This coordination strategy allows for the fastest movement for low-mass objects.*

A high-speed, accurate movement performed with a small inertia implement such as a tennis racquet tends to use a sequential coordination pattern. This means that many body segments are used in a sequence from large to small.

One biological reason this sequential coordination is most effective has to do with the mechanical properties of the muscles and tendons. Muscles and tendons have different mechanical stiffness (elasticity) at different rates of loading, this is called viscoelasticity. A muscle that is loaded (stretched or shortened) quickly behaves stiffer than if loaded slowly. Muscles also have different tension capability for the various speeds of shortening or lengthening. The faster the muscle is contracted, the less tension (force) it is able to generate, but the faster the muscle is actively lengthened (eccentric action) the greater the force the muscle can sustain. Combined these two properties encourage our bodies to naturally coordinate movements sequentially and with counter-movements, so that key muscles are first eccentrically stretched (actively elongated by acting to brake counter-movement) and immediately shortened in the intended direction of motion.

Integration Box 3.2

Viscoelastic Muscles and Tendons

Muscles and tendons behave like complex springs where a large percentage of the energy stored in stretched connective tissue can be recovered when they return to normal length. A material that has different mechanical stiffness (elasticity) based on the timing of the force application is called viscoelastic. When muscles, tendons, and bones are gradually stretched, they have low stiffness (low forces for greater elongation), but if rapidly stretched, they have high stiffness (large force for small elongation). A tensed, stiff muscle can store and recover more energy than a relaxed, compliant muscle. A similar, but extreme example of viscoelasticity is "Silly Putty". A low force applied over time makes the putty easily deformable, so it can be shaped with small forces. A rapid force application makes the putty stiff and resistant to changes in shape. Try bouncing a "Silly Putty" tennis ball or rapidly stretching a "Silly Putty" tennis string and note the rapid increase in resistance.

Take the forward swing phase of the serve for example. When the hips and torso begin their rotation forward, the upper arm lags behind due to its inertia and the fact that it is not rigidly connected to the torso. The muscles across the chest to the upper arm therefore get rapidly stretched (loaded), making the muscle stiffer, creating higher tensions in the muscle than it normally makes concentrically. Much of this elastic energy stored in the connective tissue of the muscle during the stretch can be recovered to spring the arm forward with greater force if there is minimal pause between the stretch and the shortening phases.

The faster the muscle is contracted, the less tension (force) it is able to generate, but the faster the muscle is actively lengthened (eccentric action) the greater the force the muscle can sustain.

The improvement in the performance of shortening of muscles that have been previously stretched eccentrically is substantial and is called the stretch-shortening cycle. The acceleration of a large body segment in sequential coordination contributes to a stretch-shortening cycle of the muscles of the following segment (Figure 3.5) that eccentrically act to slow its countermovement and essentially bounce into its shortening contribution. There are several mechanisms involved, beyond storage and recovery of energy in muscles and tendon, in the skilled use of stretch-shoretning cycles in coordinating movements.

The improvement in the performance of shortening of muscles that have been previously stretched eccentrically is substantial and is called the stretch-shortening cycle.

In theory the best flat tennis serve would consist of the following body segment rotations, after the preparatory movements of the backswing: extension of the legs, hip and trunk rotation, upper arm rotations, elbow/forearm rotations, and wrist rotations. This theory is generally true, but, of course, the human body is too complex for us to know exactly how all the energy transfer is accomplished, and there is some small variation in the timing of various body segments and their possible rotations. Nonetheless, many players want to

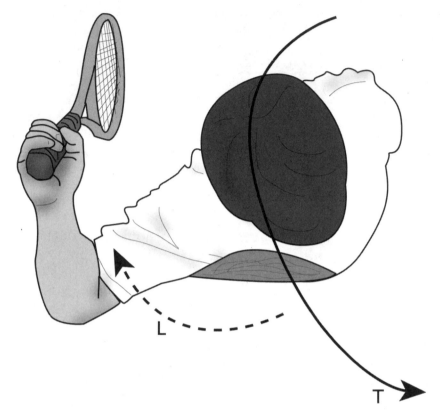

Figure 3.5 *Top view schematic of the trunk and upper arm in tennis serve where sequential coordination contributes to transfer of energy and efficient use of the shoulder and chest muscles. The forward motion of the trunk (T) creates an inertial lag (L) of the upper arm that is braked by eccentric (active lengthening) shoulder and chest muscle action, immediately followed by the shortening of the muscle.*

know which of these body rotations contribute the most to racquet head speed. Biomechanists have developed mathematical models to derive answers to this in the serve (Springings et al. 1994; Gordon & Dapena 2006). Unfortunately, the models are incomplete, and the values they derive for these segment contributions are one-dimensional and vary over the course of the serve. It is not currently possible to link the kinematics of a three-dimensional linked segment system to their contributions to multiple objectives (forward, upward, and sideward racquet motion) as in a tennis serve. Kinematics (descriptions of motion alone) does not explain the causes of the motion.

Studies of the kinetics (causes of motion based on Newton's laws or the work-energy relationship) of tennis serves are less common and also have limitations. Bahamonde (2000) reported a three-dimensional study of how angular momentum was transferred to the arm in a tennis serve. Key conclusions were that most of the angular momentum at impact was transferred to the racquet arm primarily from the trunk's somersaulting (not twisting) angular momentum. Bahamonde also agreed with Springings et al. (1994) that apparently non-contributing motions (to a one-dimensional variable such as forward racquet motion) may actually be quite important to position the body so other sources of angular momentum can be transferred.

Other kinematic and kinetic studies of the serve are consistent in showing that shoulder internal rotation motion and torques (long axis rotation of the shoulder turning the palm downward), shoulder horizontal adduction (arm horizontally across the chest), and wrist flexion are key movements in the tennis serve (Elliott et al. 1995; Fleisig et al. 2003; Van Gheluwe et al. 1987). While this is well recognized and in agreement with the common coaching opinion, it would be a mistake to attach a percentage value or overemphasize the importance of these joint movements. For example, a beginning tennis player with an immature overarm pattern uses very little of these movements because his serve resembles a pushing overarm pattern. Many people, both boys and girls, stop ovearm throwing development at less than the mature level because of inactivity or participation in non-throwing sports. Another reason to be cautious about the importance of specific body movements is that all the movements must be integrated and small variations in one action can affect the others.

Research on the coordination of the serve has shown some variety in the sequencing of the hips, trunk, and upper extremity joint actions in the serve. This parallels research on high-speed overarm throwing. Classic sequential coordination suggested that after the weight shift, pelvic rotation occurred, followed by trunk rotation. Motor development scholars called this sequential action between the pelvis and trunk "differentiated rotation" and claimed that this represented the highest level of trunk action in throwing and striking. Recent research in tennis and baseball pitching has shown that not all elite athletes used differentiated rotation. Research has also shown that there is very high abdominal and lower back muscle activation in the serve. The co-activation (activation of opposing muscles) and precise cooperation of the many muscles of the trunk provide an essential, but poorly understood, link in energy transfer from the lower extremities to the racquet arm.

Research on the coordination of the serve has shown some variety in the sequencing of the hips, trunk, and upper extremity joint actions in the serve.

Another example of the complicated picture is the observation that often peak joint rotation speeds in the serving arm are not anatomically sequential, with the typical sequence being elbow extension, wrist flexion, and then shoulder internal rotation. The key ideas in the previous point are that these are peak speeds of joint rotation (forces and initial motion occurred earlier) and that the sequential coordination may not have to be anatomically or exactly inside-out. Clearly, there are a variety of combinations of joint motions that can be used to create a tennis serve.

Biomechanics uses the idea of "degrees of freedom" to describe the number of motions that must be controlled in a linked segment system. One degree of freedom is a dimension or axis of rotation that must be controlled. A door hinge has one degree of freedom since it allows the door to swing on one plane (parallel to the floor), but not the other two. The serving arm, for example, could be said to have seven degrees of freedom (Figure 3.6). The timing and sequencing of these seven joint motions is what makes a tennis serve so complex. Some biomechanists would even argue that, expecially for the serve, the grip constitutes another degree of freedom where finger pressure can also move the racquet in the hand.

Coaches and players would love simple, easy answers to the questions of what is the best sequence and what is the most important joint motion in a flat serve. Unfortunately, the complexity of the body and individual differences makes this very unlikely. People with different strengths and flexibilities in the trunk or shoulder would likely have slightly different sequential coordination patterns of the seven or eight degrees of freedom in their serve. A good final example of the contribution and coordination problem relates to what is commonly called the "wrist snap" in a flat serve.

For decades players believed that a vigorous wrist action or wrist snap was essential to a high-speed serve. Once high-speed film and video cameras were able to document what actually occurred in the flat serve, what was seen was not exactly overwhelming confirmation. What is commonly called the wrist

Figure 3.6 *The seven degrees of freedom (distinct joint rotations) of the serving arm represents a very complex linked segment system. Precise coordination of all these motions are necessary for a successful tennis serve/stroke.*

snap is a combination of forearm pronation and two wrist motions (flexion and ulnar deviation). Pronation is rotating the forearm so the palm of the hand faces down or back, wrist flexion in rotating the hand in the direction of the palm, and ulnar deviation is a small tilting or sideward hand rotation toward the little finger. Forearm pronation is especially important in the flat serve because this joint rotation helps square the racquet face with the ball that contributes to greater ball speed than spin.

What is commonly called the wrist snap is a combination of forearm pronation and two wrist motions (flexion and ulnar deviation).

These three joint motions occur very close to impact and continue through impact, so there are serious data analysis problems that make velocity calculations subject to large errors (Knudson and Bahamonde, 2001). Although, these motions have been estimated to account for about 35 percent of the racquet speed near impact (Elliott et al. 1995), remember that experimental errors or interactions of other joint rotations could even make these motions counterproductive in another sequence of segment motions in a serve. Mistiming of shoulder or elbow motion could allow for pronation to be pointing the racquet in the wrong direction. Even if the pronation and wrist flexion motion were just being initiated at impact and not generating much racquet speed by themselves, the fact that they are not collapsing in the opposite direction allows these limited motions to transfer energy from other motions. It is likely that forearm pronation is a key joint action in the flat serve because it helps move and square up the racquet face with the ball, which is critical for the creation of greater ball speed than spin.

A good example of this kind of passive effect is throwing a baseball. It is hard to believe that the fingers of the throwing hand don't contribute to the speed a baseball is thrown since the ball is held in the fingertips. Ultra-high speed imaging studies of baseball throwing show that the fingers do not flex (bend forward) during release, but are actually extending. The vigorous push off on the ball pushes the fingers into a more extended position, but the fingers are still transferring a lot of energy and motion to the baseball. Just like it would be incorrect to say that the fingers don't help speed up the baseball from their apparent lack of forward motion, it is also incorrect to say that limited wrist flexion or elbow extension motion near impact means they contribute little to racquet speed. Coaches and players should be cautioned that a lack of apparent motion (kinematics) is purely descriptive, and it can't thus be inferred that lack of motion implies no active or causative role in the transfer of energy to the racquet. Easy answers and standard percentage contributions of various body segments to serve speed are just not possible.

Hitting Out: Optimal Projection

Optimal Projection is an important principle in the flat serve because the margin for error is so small in the vertical plane. The previous section mentioned how the racquet path in the flat serve as seen from above (horizontal plane) closely matches the direction of the target. The angle the ball should be hit in the vertical plane can be seen from a side view of the serve and is usually defined as the angle of ball motion relative to horizontal (Figure 3.7). Many players think the serve should be hit on a downward initial trajectory because the serve is often hit hard and appears to fly on a slightly downward trajectory to the casual eye. As we will see below, this is not always true, especially now that players have powerful, larger-head, high-tech racquets.

Figure 3.7 *The initial trajectory of the ball of a tennis serve in the vertical plane can be described by the angle of the ball velocity to the horizontal.*

Early high-speed film studies (early to mid-twentieth century) of the tennis serves of advanced male and female players showed that an initial angle of ball flight usually between 8 degrees below horizontal up to 10 degrees above. This research on the serves of skilled tennis players showed that the ball was hit very near the peak of the racquet motion, while the racquet was moving upward or transitioning to downward. Only very high-speed serves could initially be hit slightly downward and still clear the net and land in the service box. Most beginners and recreational players served the ball with small initial upward trajectories. The typical windows of successful flat serve angles depend on the height of contact (player's height) and skill (ball speed and spin).

Most skilled players could hit flat serves 100 to 120 mph with the small, wooden racquets used years ago. Today it is not uncommon to see men and women touring pros hitting 120 to 150 mph serves during tournaments. Although gravity and air resistance have not changed, the substantial increase in serve speed might indicate that the optimal windows for ball projection in the modern serve have changed. It appears that the successful initial angles of flat serves has shifted downward, but only slightly.

Short or lower skill level players who typically are hitting flat serves slower than 70 mph will still be hitting the ball on an upward or flat initial trajectory, and will "net" serves hit more than a couple degrees below horizontal. Taller more advanced players will be able to hit flat serves (80 to 110 mph) horizontally or down to about 8 degrees below the horizontal. Very skilled servers that can hit flat serves over 120 mph may be successful with initial trajectories 8 to 10 degrees below the horizontal. So most players should strive to achieve the feeling of hitting up through the ball on the flat serve so the initial ball trajectory is near horizontal. Only at more advanced levels can the ball be hit initially downward on a flat serve, and even then not sharply.

The substantial increase in serve speed might indicate that the optimal windows for ball projection in the modern serve have changed. It appears that the successful initial angles of flat serves has shifted downward, but only slightly.

Integration Box 3.3

Gender Differences in the Serve

Currently women's professional tennis is enjoying surging popularity because of an influx of talented women players and decreased interest in the big-serve men's game. For decades, motor development studies have documented more females with lower level throwing technique than males. In general, adult females have about two-thirds of the strength of similar (age and training) males. Are women destined to have inferior serving technique than men or is this a cultural phenomenon? While there is not a lot of research on male/female technique differences in tennis strokes (there is in some movements like throwing, running, and jumping), there are descriptive studies of female players, and there is enough anecdotal evidence to support the conclusions that women likely serve as well as men, and with very few differences in technique. It's an interesting exercise converting performance statistics (such as serve speed or a strength measure) of men and women into relative terms. Normalizing serve speed to height or strength-to-weight usually puts trained women's performance scores very close to men's. Many gender differences seem to be more related to participation than biological differences.

SLICE SERVE

The slice serve technique is a subtle adjustment of the flat serve to create a combination of an angled racquet face and sideward racquet path through impact. Racquet motion to the right or a more angled racquet face creates ball sidespin that makes the ball curve through the air and bounce to the left. Coaches typically use cues like "brush" or hit the "far" side of the ball to get this image across to players. This section will explain what the research on the slice serve tells us about the coordination used to create a slice serve.

Brushing Right: Coordinaton and Transfer

Motion of the racquet to the right in a slice serve comes at a cost of a decrease in ball speed toward the service box. In elite tennis players, slice serves may have ball speeds between 70 and 80 percent of flat serves, but the racquet is usually swung about as fast (90 and 95 percent) as a flat serve. This high racquet speed is needed to create the sidespin and still retain good ball speed toward the court. It is a common error for beginning tennis players to slow racquet speeds (down to even 40 to 50 percent of their first serve) when trying to maximize accuracy with a slice second serve. It appears that slice serves are hit with somewhat similar initial angles to the horizontal. Since sidespin is the pri-

In elite tennis players, slice serves may have ball speeds between 70 and 80 percent of flat serves, but the racquet is usually swung about as fast (90 and 95 percent) as a flat serve.

mary spin created, the lift forces created on the ball create more sideward motion than downward motion that would affect the angle of projection. Let's look at what coordination seems to be used to create this fast brush of the ball.

Unfortunately, few three-dimensional studies of the slice serve have focused on the timing and coordination of upper extremity joint actions used by tennis players. The following observations are based more on qualitative observations of high-speed video and other published biomechanical variables.

Slice serves may be created by a slightly more angled (1 to 4 degrees) racquet face at impact, but the more consistent difference is the path of the racquet through the ball. Flat serves tend to have the racquet moving through the ball toward the service box while slice serves have racquet paths through the ball 10 to 20 degrees to the right this direct path (Chow et al. 2003). A player wanting to hit a slice serve toward the center service line would likely swing the racquet through the ball as illustrated in Figure 3.1a. Skilled servers can vary the racquet angle and racquet path through the ball to create a variety of ball speed and sidespin combinations.

The timing of the joint actions of the arm must be precisely timed to create the speed, direction, and racquet alignment to meet the ball (Figure 3.8). It is not clear from the research exactly how the timing and motion of specific joints vary to create a slice rather than a flat serve. Logically, one could speculate that shoulder internal rotation and pronation might have to be delayed and closer to impact than a flat serve. These rotations tend to square up the racquet face if the other joint actions occur in their typical sequence. Unfortunately, there are geometric and technical problems in measuring these very fast long axis rotations in movements like the serve (Gordon and Dapena, in press). Improvements in biomechanics research technology might be needed before these more subtle aspects of the tennis slice serve are documented.

One thing is certain in creating spin in all tennis strokes is that this "brushing" of the ball is made by a combination of joint motions occurring through impact. Trying to create a "wrist flick" in a particular direction at the moment

Figure 3.8 *A slice serve at impact creates primarily ball sidespin by an angled racquet face and a high-racquet head speed. The racquet angle and motion hitting through the ball slightly to the right is a result of a complex combination of shoulder internal rotation, elbow extension, forearm pronation, and wrist flexion.*

 One thing is certain in creating spin in all tennis strokes is that this "brushing" of the ball is made by a combination of joint motions occurring through impact. Trying to create a "wrist flick" in a particular direction at the moment of impact would not work and would be a incorrect prescription.

of impact would not work and would be a incorrect prescription that would usually result only in poor ball speed and spin. A player must stroke vigorously through the ball with the angled racquet face, not try to "brush" the ball to the extent that he is trying to peel felt off the ball.

Twist Serve

The twist serve is a spin serve that has two advantages over the flat and slice server—greater topspin and a different bounce. The topspin helps the ball curve downward, decreasing the risk of hitting past the service line. The higher and sideward (opposite of a slice serve) bounce of a twist serve is particularly effective against lower level players who are not used to returning these serves. As was noted in Chapter Two, there are two approaches to creating this spin on the ball, with one likely exposing the lower back to a greater risk of injury. Like the slice serve, there is little research on the twist serve on which to make precise recommendations on the best coordination of arm motions for the serve.

Brushing Up: Coordination and Transfer

Studies of the twist serve do agree with the coaching opinion that the racquet should brush upward and across the ball (to the right). Research has confirmed that the toss in the twist serve is less forward (into the court) and closer to the head than the hitting shoulder. The ball is usually impacted at a lower point to allow for the upward motion of the racquet. These adjustments in the toss allows for more upward and to the right motion of the racquet while striking the ball (Figure 3.9). The sideward and upward components of racquet head speed cannot be great if the arm is nearing its range of motion limits, slowing the racquet as it changes direction. Remember that it is an important not to let these shifts in toss placement be exaggerated. Too much to the left or backward may tip off your opponent or require your back to arch/lean, placing uneven stresses in your back.

The safest way to create upward racquet velocity appears to be emphasizing vigorous leg extension, rather than back arching and flexion. Some research has reported up to 20 more degrees of knee bend in preparation for twist serves compared to flat serves (Lo et al. 2004). Players should be warned that excessive lower back arching and lateral lean (leaning toward the tossing arm) preparing for twist serves place potentially dangerous loads on the spine. A more upward arm action must also be added to the upward leg drive to create a good twist serve.

Figure 3.9 *A racquet must be tilted a little from vertical and be moving upward to create the ball topspin in a twist serve. The toss can only be slightly to the left and behind of a regular toss to disguise the serve and reduce strain on the lower back.*

It is also unclear exactly how the timing and motion of joints of the arm create a twist serve. Logically, greater upward and sideward motion of the racquet would be created by increased elbow extension, wrist flexion, and ulnar deviation. There is some support for this theory. Coutinho et al. (2004) reported greater elbow extensor muscle activation in the twist than the flat serve of an

THE SERVE

The technique used by Pete Sampras for a slice serve is illustrated in Figure 3.10 below. This perspective does not allow a good view of the large circular backswing, but the photos do highlight several strengths of other preparatory motions. Sampras effectively uses a platform or foot-back stance serve technique. Then there are the strengths of his deep knee bend, a straight (not arched) back, and good alignment of his upper arm with the trunk in his preparation. Some coaches use the cue of the "trophy position" to give players a positive visual image of this point (photo 2) in the serve. The powerful upward motion of Pete's body out of this stretch-shortening cycle in the lower body transfers energy up through the trunk to the racquet arm. The excel-

lent sequential coordination of Pete's trunk and arm action is evident in nearly 180 degree change in shoulder external rotation from photo 2 to photo 3. The upward leg drive and trunk rotation create an inertial lag from the weight of the arm and racquet. This creates a powerful stretch-shortening cycle in the shoulder internal rotator muscles. Shoulder internal rotation appears to be one of the most important contributors to racquet speed in the tennis serve. At impact (photo 4) you can see that the coordinated actions of the shoulder, elbow, and wrist have resulted in a fast and angled racquet face at impact for a slice serve. Sampras finishes his serve with a long follow-through around his body and begins approaching the net. He shows excellent coordination and dynamic balance by integrating the forward and upward service motion with his subsequent approach to the net. The other principles related to the serve, such as optimal projection, are also well performed by Sampras but it is difficult to observe them from this viewing angle.

Figure 3.10 *The slice serve of Pete Sampras. (Sequence images taken by Lance Jeffery and used with permission of USTA High Performance.)*

The safest way to create upward racquet velocity appears to be emphasizing vigorous leg extension, rather than back arching and flexion. Some research has reported up to 20 more degrees of knee bend in preparation for twist serves compared to flat serves.

advanced player. It is also likely that the long axis of the racquet be angled more to the vertical at impact with the ball (Figure 3.9), although this has not been reported in biomechanical studies. Coaches and players must wait for more research, focusing on these general guidelines and practice to refine the twist serve. It is also very important to remember that, like the slice serve, high-racquet head speeds are also needed in the twist serve. It may take considerable practice for some players to pick up the right arm motions and racquet path, and to time this correctly with a slightly lower and overhead ball toss.

Higher Arc: Optimal Projection

The upward racquet motion in the twist serve contributes to a higher initial ball trajectory than the flat or slice serves. There is very little experimental data on which to suggest what are the typical technique differences for skilled players. Coaches and players should just focus on creating the upward brushing of the ball by the racquet strings. Future research might provide some general guidelines on what racquet alignments and motions through the ball are most effective.

SUMMARY AND MATCH POINTS

Biomechanically, there are three main tennis serves based on the amount of speed and spin imparted on the ball: flat, slice, and twist. A flat serve maximizes speed and minimizes spin, but usually has some topspin. The slice has primarily sidespin, and the twist has primarily topspin. The essential mechanical principles in creating a high-speed (flat) serve are the use of at least a continental grip, vigorous knee bend and extension, sequential coordination, and upward and outward hitting action. Initial ball trajectories for most players are close to horizontal, with downward ball trajectories only possible for very high-speed serves. The slice serve is created by similar racquet speed as a flat serve, but with a trajectory about 10 to 20 degrees to the right of the target. The twist serve is created by an upward brush through the ball. The safest technique for this serve is to emphasize leg and arm action over trunk arch/lean.

Match Points

- Continental and eastern grips are the best for serving because they allow free wrist motions and effective creation of ball spin.

- Much of the energy of a good serve comes from the vigorous knee bend and extension in the service action.

- Use the foot-up technique to increase vertical forces, ball speed, and topspin, while use of the foot-back technique favors balance and horizontal force production to rush the net.

- All serves create ball spin, but a flat serve minimizes ball spin and maximizes ball speed.

- Swing just as hard for a slice serve because the angled racquet face and motion that create spin come at a cost (20-30%) of ball speed toward the service box.

- Create the upward racquet motion through the ball on a twist serve by using knee bend and extension rather that arching your back.

Chapter Four

BIOMECHANICS OF THE FOREHAND

"In fact, the forehand is one of the most misunderstood strokes in the game."—Vic Braden

Often the forehand is the most natural of all the tennis strokes and Braden is right that many players gloss over the subtleties of the forehand. Research has identified some biomechanical commonalities of all tennis groundstrokes and provides important information on forehand technique adaptations. This chapter will look at the general skill issues of tennis groundstrokes, with specific discussion of forehand techniques. Key groundstroke and forehand issues are grips, preparation and footwork, stance, stroke, and follow-through.

GRIPS

Tennis forehands use a variety of grips that allow the hand and wrist considerable motion. If you look at the palm of your hand, you can see the flexion creases in your skin. The handle of the racquet is angled across your hand along the general, diagonal direction of these lines. Whatever style of grip you use in the forehand, continental, eastern, or western, this use of the hand allows for a strong and yet mobile grasp of the tennis racquet. These grips are different from a power grip (90° across hand) that maximizes grip strength.

Different styles of tennis grips, naturally influence how much specific hand and wrist motions will be the easiest to use in the forehand. This will affect the joints you use for Coordination and Transfer of Energy in your strokes, as well as provide natural strengths and weakness for various bounces and spins you

Different styles of tennis grips, naturally influence how much specific hand and wrist motions will be the easiest to use in the forehand. This will affect the joints you use for Coordination and Transfer of Energy in your strokes.

must handle during play. A western style grip essentially puts the hand under the racquet handle, so wrist flexion near impact in a forehand helps create an upward brushing action effective for creating topspin (Figure 4.1a). The eastern forehand grip has the hand behind the handle making it effective for increasing forward racquet speed, resisting the shock of impact and accommodating a wide variety of heights of impact (Figure 4.1b). A continental grip has the hand shifted toward the top of the handle. This often tends to "open" (angle upward) the racquet face in a forehand, unless the player uses more shoulder internal rotation or forearm pronation. Notice that the interaction of other arm motions allows the continental grip, which is half way between the

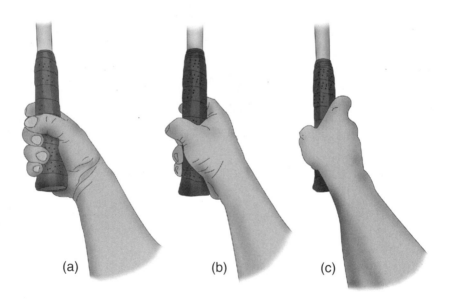

(a)   (b)   (c)

Figure 4.1 *Forehand grip styles affect the positioning and motions of the racquet created by hand/arm actions. A western grip allows wrist flexion to contribute to upward racquet motion for topspin (a), an eastern grip allows wrist flexion to create more forward racquet motion (b), while a continental grip also allows wrist flexion to create forward racquet motion if long-axis rotations of the arm backward help square up the racquet face (c).*

eastern forehand and backhand grips to serve as a forehand or a backhand grip. Rather than switching grips, a player using a continental grip can practice small adjustments in arm joint actions to keep the racquet face positioned correctly for impact.

The coaching wisdom about forehand grips and their strategic consequences has changed over the years. Eastern grips were advocated because of the strong hand position and ability to hit balls bouncing at all heights. Although players have always used continental and western forehand grips, they were typically not taught. Today most coaches realize that the grip is more a matter of style and a player can choose the forehand grip he finds most comfortable. Players and coaches need to realize that these choices have biomechanical and strategic strengths and weaknesses. Continental grips are good for low bouncing balls and hitting backspin on the forehand side. The grip tends to be weaker than the other two and may make it difficult for high-bouncing shots. The eastern grip forehand is stronger and the most adaptable to impact points at different heights or distances from the body. The western grip may the strongest and easy for weaker players to use. Western forehands accommodate high bounces well, but may be difficult to execute on very low bounces.

 Today most coaches realize that the grip is more a matter of style and players can choose the forehand grip they find most comfortable. Players and coaches need to realize that these choices have biomechanical and strategic strengths and weaknesses.

Before we leave grips it is important to revisit the myth that a firm grip is essential to high-speed tennis strokes mentioned in Chapter 2. The duration of ball impact (4-5 ms) is just too short for hand forces to significantly increase the momentum of the tennis racquet and ball. Players can use extra grip forces, but the tension in the forearm muscles stiffens the wrist, tending to decrease wrist motion that could add to ball speed or spin. Measurements of hand forces in strokes shows that grip forces in the forward swing stay small (30 to 60 percent of maximum grip) and only increase just before impact (1/20th second). Whatever grip style is used by a player, he should focus on gripping enough to control the racquet before and after impact.

PREPARATION AND FOOTWORK

Optimal performance in tennis groundstrokes, like the forehand, requires good preparatory movements and footwork to intercept the ball. Great stroke technique is useless if the player cannot get into position. The two key elements of this preparation are the split step and the footwork used to move to intercept the ball.

Good groundstrokes truly begin with the preparatory movements to help a player quickly react and move to an opponent's shot. The technique is called a split step (Figure 4.2). A split step is essentially a hop or jump into a ready position. Split steps create stretch-shortening cycle (Chapter 3) muscle actions in the leg extensors as the player lands in the ready position, so he can maximize his quickness to intercept the ball. This is consistent with the principles of Force and Time and Balance and Inertia. The stretch-shortening cycle actions of the leg muscles are used to create high initial muscle forces because the time to create motion must be minimized, and the relatively shallow countermovement and moderate size of the base of support make it easy for the player to make initial movements of the body. By stopping the body motion of

Figure 4.2 *Skilled players perform a split step by hopping into a short, quick leg bend. This creates stretch-shortening cycle muscle actions in the leg extensors to facilitate a high-force, quick push off to intercept the ball.*

recovery to split step, a player maximizes his ability to move in any direction. The split step is the ideal court movement transition technique.

A player side-stepping back from a wide forehand typically strives to bisect the possible angles of the opponent's potential shots (Figure 4.3). If the player has not reached the ideal recovery position, he still should square up his feet with the opponent and synchronize his split step (SS) to the opponent's strike of the ball. The key to maximizing the quickness of the reaction is to keep the hop and bend in the leg joints small and fast. Stretch-shortening cycle actions are most effective when they minimize the time of the action and delays between the countermovement and the reaction. Once the player is skilled at timing and quickly bouncing out of a split step, then he can work on refining his footwork and movement to the ball.

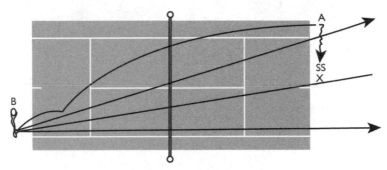

Figure 4.3 *Player A shuffling back to recover from a wide forehand normally strives to get to the middle of the possible angles of return (X), but should, however, split step (SS) as the opponent (B) hits the ball even if he is not at his ideal recovery point.*

Traditionally it has been taught that players should slide for balls close and run to balls hit far from their split-step position. This rule-of-thumb promotes energy efficient movement for nearby shots, but is not specific as to the best footwork to use in running forward or sideward to distant shots. The best footwork to use out of the split step to run various distances and directions is less clear. Surprisingly, there is not a lot of research on this topic, so there are only a few studies of football, base running, volleyball, and tennis (Lamond et al. 1996; Bragg and Andriacchi, 2001) to guide us. The focus will be on quick lateral motion because the majority of tennis movements are sideways and not very far (less than 5 meters).

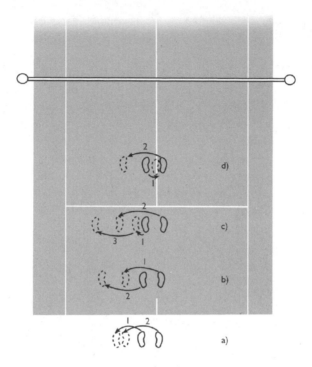

Figure 4.4 *Initial foot motion for the four techniques of lateral motion footwork. Slide step (a), cross-over step (b), jab cross-over (c), and the gravity step (d).*

The main lateral motion footwork techniques are the slide step where the foot nearest the target is moved first (Figure 4.4a) and three variations that transition to running: the cross-over step (4.4b), jab cross-over step (4.4c), and the gravity step (4.4d). In the cross-over step, the player brings the foot from the opposite side and crosses it over in the intended direction of motion. The jab cross-over begins with a very short step with the same side foot before crossing over with the opposite foot. The gravity step essentially picks up the near foot and draws it under the body to let gravity and body lean assist initial motion before placing the foot down and crossing over with the other foot.

 The slide step is the slowest, but there are minimal differences between the speeds of movement for the three cross-over footwork techniques.

The research is fairly consistent that the slide step is the slowest and this is why this would be an appropriate technique for submaximal movement to play groundstrokes close to the body. The results of most of these studies indicate that there are minimal differences between the speeds of movement for the three cross-over footwork techniques. In a short (less than 5 meters) movement, each of the three will likely have times within a tenth of a second and typical variation across strokes. If a coach or player prefers one technique over the other, consistent practice should help the player improve his footwork and quickness to the ball. Cues can emphasize quick foot motion and vigorous push off from the opposite foot.

STANCES

Once the player is in position for a groundstroke, there is a variety of stances from which the stroke can be executed. The stance used affects how the body can be used to create the stroke (Coordination and Transfer) and how it can transition into the recovery for the next stroke (Balance and Inertia). Stances fall on a continuum between an open stance and a closed stance. A open stance has the players feet facing the target (Figure 4.5a), a square stance has the body turned to align the feet with the target (Figure 4.5b), and a closed stance has the front foot moved beyond the square stance position along the target line.

> **The advantages of the square stance forehand are the ability to use leg drive to shift body weight forward and transfer this energy through the hips, trunk, arm and the shot.**

A stance is most stable in the direction where the base of support is widest and, conversely, is easiest to initiate movement in the directions where the base of support is more narrow. A player's base of support is the area between his supporting limbs (foot or feet). A square stance, for example, has the base of support elongated toward the target (Figure 4.6). This maximizes the stability and ability to shift body weight in this direction, but motion to the side quickly leaves the base of support so it is easier to fall into locomotion in these directions.

The advantages of the square stance forehand are the ability to use leg drive to shift body weight forward and transfer this energy through the hips, trunk, arm and the shot. In theory, this means that the square stance could have

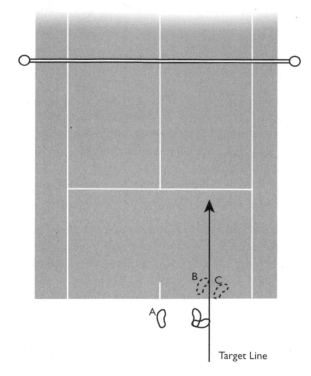

Figure 4.5 *Striking stances are classified on a continuum based on foot position relative to the target. An open stance has both feet square with the target (a), while a square stance has the feet aligned with the target line (b), and a closed stance has the front foot beyond the target line (c).*

greater ball speed and accuracy than the open stance. These benefits are believed to come from an elongated racquet path toward the target, but have not been confirmed by research (Knudson and Bahamonde, 1999). More controlled research is needed to examine this controversy, but it is clear that each stance is effective and the path of the racquet head in most forehands near impact tends to be more circular than linear. The disadvantage of a square stance is that the lateral recovery for this shot is farther than for the semi-open or open stance forehand. A player finishing this forehand with most of his body weight near the front foot may even have to bring the rear foot to the side or forward to stop and begin recovery for the next shot.

An open stance forehand has much of the base of support and body weight closer to the recovery point than a square stance forehand. This improves the recovery time for most forehands and can improve the time to reach the oppo-

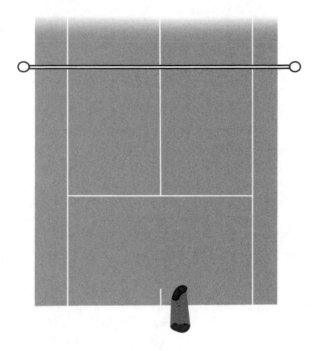

Figure 4.6 *A square stance forehand has an elongated base of support in line with the target. This increases stability and ability to shift weight forward into the stroke.*

site sideline by about a tenth of a second. The disadvantage of the open stance forehand is that the stroke relies more on body angular motion to create racquet speed. This does create more of a glancing racquet path through impact that increases the accuracy demands for a successful stroke. The intermediate group in the Knudson and Bahamonde (1999) study had less consistent racquet paths in the open stance forehand than the square stance.

Many tennis instruction books describe the square stance as using primarily linear momentum, and the open stance as using angular momentum. In reality, all tennis strokes use a combination of both, but it could be said that one

 An open stance forehand improves the recovery time for most forehands and can improve the time to reach the opposite sideline by about a tenth of a second.

tends to favor one source more than another. The important ideas about momentum are that it is a kinetic quantity, that it is proportional to the impulse (forces and duration of their action), and it is transferable. In other words, you can't see momentum unless your eyes can weigh objects and do multiplication at the same time. The apparently moderate-speed forward motion of the legs and trunk may have considerable linear momentum because of their large masses, and a very fast rotation of a small body segment may have only moderate angular momentum because of its small inertia (moment of inertia) about that axis of rotation. What is important is that tennis players use both kinds of momentum and transfer one form to another to drive tennis strokes. The essentially linear momentum of falling into a split step results in angular momentum in the joints of the legs. The forward motion of a weight shift has linear momentum that can be transferred into angular momentum of the hip, trunk, and racquet arm. The coordination and transfer of energy of these motions is affected by the stance used.

Emergency forehands and many backhands are often hit from a closed stance. In general, this is theoretically less desirable than a square stance based on the principle of Coordination and Transfer of Energy. The coupling of forward motion to hip rotation is one of the first key transfers of energy in many tennis strokes, but the positioning the forward hip forward of the target line tends to limit the rotation that can occur horizontally around this hip. This limits some of the transfer of energy or angular momentum from the legs to the trunk.

STROKE

The forehand stroke itself occurs continuously with the preparation, footwork, and stance. This section will describe the forehand stroking action itself and outline key points showing how the stroking techniques are integrated with the previous technique points. The backswing, forward stroke with accompanying spin generation, and follow-through are examined. The primary principles to be applied in shaping your stroke are Range of Motion, Coordination and Transfer of Energy, and Optimal Projection.

Backswing. The racquet backswing usually begins during the steps to intercept the ball. Traditional strokes had the forehand backswing being relatively straight toward the back fence. This naturally results in players using a small loop (Plagenhoef, 1970). This tendency to take the racquet back higher and then allow it to drop to create this loop backswing (Figure 4.7) has been controversial in instructional circles over the years. The size or range of motion of

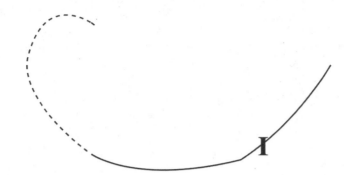

Figure 4.7 *A side view of the loop (_ _ _) and forward swing (___) portions of a topspin forehand. Note there are two upward paths of the racquet in the forward swing—one to intercept the ball and a second adjustment just before impact (**I**) to increase the topspin on the stroke. This two-phase pattern is common in the forehands and backhands of advanced players even though it is not commonly a technique point taught to players.*

the loop varies, but the continuous motion allows for kinetic energy of the racquet to be created as the player is essentially setting up for the forward stroke. Some players prefer large loops while other players prefer smaller ones. Either is effective, although large loops may be more difficult to adapt stroke timing to unexpected bounces or ball speeds.

 Some players prefer large loops while other players prefer smaller ones. Either is effective, although large loops may be more difficult to adapt stroke timing to unexpected bounces or ball speeds.

This loop does not appear to short-circuit the sequential coordination and stretch-shortening cycle sequence of strokes. First, the racquet speeds of the backswings should be relatively slow. Second, the rapid motion of the hips and trunk creates enough inertial lag in the racquet arm to create active stretches

 Coaches and players should only adjust the backswing if they are drifting toward an extreme that is creating a problem with timing or stroke speed.

of the key muscles in the forehand. Consistent and early racquet preparation is clearly more important than a particular tempo or size of loop. Coaches and players should only adjust the backswing if they are drifting toward an extreme that is creating a problem with timing or stroke speed.

Forward swing—flat. The forward swing of the racquet is created along a path timed to intercept the ball and create either predominantly topspin or backspin. A flat forehand that maximizes ball speed is possible with a gradual (10 to 40 degrees) upward racquet motion (to remove the incident ball's topspin), but most players create ball spin to aid in shot control and achieve a particular tactical objective. The racquet face at impact must be very close to vertical (less than 10 degrees) on most groundstrokes, with subtle adjustments near vertical for very high-spin strokes (Figure 4.8 and 4.9).

Bounce Off A Moving Racquet

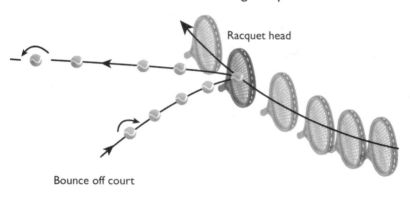

Racquet head

Bounce off court

Figure 4.8 *Schematic of hitting a topspin with the ball on the rise. Note that the racquet face is nearly vertical or slightly closed (angled down) at impact. (Used with permission from Brody, Cross, and Lindsey [2002].)*

Forward swing—topspin. It is more difficult to reverse the spin of the ball, so topspin forehands require fast racquet head speeds and fairly steep racquet paths through impact. This is usually achieved by a gradual upward stroke path matched to the ball trajectory followed by a rapid increase in racquet path just before impact (Figure 4.7). This sharp increase in trajectory to create topspin has been reported in both forehands and backhands. Recall that there are technical problems in getting accurate data about racquet velocity near

Figure 4.9 *Ultra high-speed (6,000 frames per second) image of a topspin forehand. Note the slightly closed racquet face at impact that is forced square by the recoil from the off-center impact. (Images courtesy of the International Tennis Federation.)*

impacts, but in general it appears that topspin forehands have a racquet path through impact between 35 and 50 degrees above the horizontal (Knudson and Elliott, 2004), while a topspin lob would be between 50 and 70 degrees.

 It is more difficult to reverse the spin of the ball, so topspin forehands require fast racquet head speeds and fairly steep racquet paths through impact.

Some recent studies have reported flatter racquet paths when hitting moderate topspin strokes off balls with small amounts of incident spin (Blackwell and Knudson, 2005; Knudson and Blackwell, 2005). The racquet face at impact tends to be aligned vertically or slightly closed (pointing down less than 10 degrees to the vertical). Racquet motion is more influential in creating ball spin than minor changes in racquet head alignment (Cross, 2005). Figure 4.9 shows two images taken from ultra high-speed video (6,000 frames per second) of a topspin forehand hit slightly off-center. Note the racquet face is square or slightly closed at impact. Also notice how the racquet slows down and it is still being pressed into the players hand even after the ball has left the strings.

 Topspin forehands have a racquet path through impact between 35 and 50 degrees above the horizontal, while a topspin lob would be between 50 and 70 degrees.

Advantage Box 4.1: Heavy Ball

Playing against a much better player can be a humbling experience. They seem to place the ball deep and away from you on every shot, and turn your own power against you. Groppel (1992) notes that this feeling of an opponent's groundstrokes overpowering your racquet is called hitting a "solid or heavy" ball. Balls cannot gain mass and get heavier (even if they pick up some clay), but advanced players do hit shots with both high-speed and spin. Remember that these two variables tend to be inversely related, but advanced players have the strength and skill to create much more racquet speed and use the sweetspot of the racquet to create more ball speed and spin than less skilled players are used to dealing with. Their strokes can't break the laws of physics or violate the speed/spin trade-off, but they have become very good at creating both ball speed and spin to an opponent's disadvantage. I recommend Groppel's (1992) discussion of factors you can work on to hit more offensive or "heavy" groundstrokes. For example, advanced players are good at hitting groundstrokes at all heights and often intercept the ball sooner (forward in the court and often as the ball is rising). This allows for a more aggressive return because some of the greater kinetic energy of the ball can be used and because of the decreased distance and time the ball travels to the opponent. Hitting the ball at a higher position allows for a more aggressive stroke angle (flatter) that will slow down less on the way to the opponent.

The arm coordination to produce an upward racquet path can use all arm joints. Classic technique tended to be dominated by shoulder motions. This style used the strong chest and shoulder muscles to drive the stroke, with forearm and wrist muscles serving primarily as stabilizers of the racquet. The more sequential coordination that is often called the "modern" forehand adds elbow flexion and wrist rotation (flexion or radial deviation) to assist in the creation of racquet speed and upward motion (Ariel and Braden, 1979; Elliott et al. 1989a). The classic technique has the advantage of greater potential for accuracy and control given the smaller number of degrees of freedom that must be controlled, while the sequential technique has the advantage of potentially higher racquet speed from the greater number of segment rotations used. (See

Classic technique tended to be dominated by shoulder motions. The more sequential coordination that is often called the "modern" forehand adds elbow flexion and wrist rotation to assist in the creation of racquet speed and upward motion.

the previous section on grips to review how grip style affects the combinations of arm joint rotations that are used in the forehand.)

Forward swing—backspin. Players hitting high-bouncing balls or trying to keep the ball deep and low to an opponent often use stroke paths that create ball backspin. This spin is easier to create because the ball is already spinning in this direction and the stroke path is assisted by gravity. Loop backswing for backspin strokes tend to be smaller so that the racquet preparation easily transitions into the forward and downward stroke path.

Backspin groundstrokes typically have downward stroke paths that are between 10 and 40 degrees below the horizontal (Knudson and Elliott, 2004). The racquet face at impact in a backspin forehand may be open (angled upward), but again this angle is very small (less than 10 degrees) and typically should not be exaggerated by players. Remember that the racquet speed and path are more influential in creating spin than small changes in the angle of the racquet. A drop shot requires a severe, downward racquet path that may even be slowing the racquet speed up to impact. This allows the player to disguise the shot from the opponent and still create a high and soft shot, with heavy backspin.

Backspin groundstrokes typically have downward stroke paths that are between 10 and 40 degrees below the horizontal.

The stroke paths discussed affect the ball spin and ball vertical and forward speed, but there is another direction of groundstroke control. Side-to-side control in tennis is commonly called a down-the-line or cross-court stroke. The mechanism for this optimal projection to adjust shots in this direction appears to be minute adjustments in the timing of the stroke to achieve an angle of the racquet face at impact (Blievernicht, 1968). So hitting a cross-court forehand

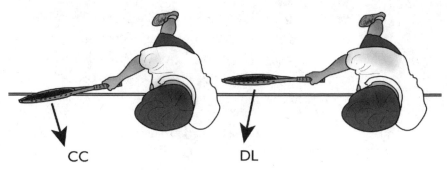

CC   DL

Figure 4.10 *Side-to-side directional control (CC: cross-court, DL: down-the-line) of groundstrokes is usually achieved by timing the stroke to angle the racquet face toward the target, rather than major adjustments of the wrist or arm joints. (Adapted from Blievernicht, 1968).*

(Figure 4.10) does not require any biomechanical adjustments in stroke technique, just a slightly earlier or faster swing to angle the racquet face more to the left. Similarly, down-the-line strokes tend to be impacted slightly later with the racquet face pointing slightly to the right. Minute adjustment in the angle of the racquet face must be made to accommodate the trajectory and speed of the ball, court location, target, and if the hitting on the run. Hitting on the run or making a large change in the direction of the ball requires considerable racquet speed at impact.

FOLLOW-THROUGH

The follow-through in the forehand varies with the purpose of the shot and according to the style of the player. Topspin forehands finish higher, gradually slowing forward and around the body. Players with compact, open stance topspin strokes tend to have a more circular follow-through around the body. Players using a square stance can elongate the follow-through more forward. A long follow-through that gradually slows the arm is important for three reasons. First, a long follow-through reduces the risk of injury (see Chapter 2). Second, performance is improved by keeping maximum racquet speed near impact—in other words, not slowing down through impact. Third, the stroking through anticipated impact may promote accuracy because, if there is

 A long follow-through that gradually slows the arm is important to reduce the risk of injury and to assist in keeping maximum racquet speed near impact.

Integration Box 4.1

Modern Racquets and the Modern Forehand

Improvements in racquet design and materials have increased the speed of the game and influenced technique. Advanced players of every era have always hit open stance forehands, but in the past they were almost exclusively used as emergency shots. The small wooden racquets did not have the power or "forgiveness" in nonsweetspot impacts to allow for less precise strokes. Open stance forehands have now become the most common forehand on all surfaces, and it is common in coaching circles to talk about the modern forehand. The trend is real, but students of the game will know that unusual stroke techniques and styles have existed since the beginning of the sport. Biomechanics researchers reported the existence of more circular, sequential, multi-segment forehands decades ago (Ariel and Braden, 1979; Elliott et al. 1989a). More important than trendy names is an understanding of the strengths and weakness of stroke techniques, so you can improve your game and break down that of your opponent. Sports engineers are constantly making improvements in racquets that are aimed at improving peformance or reducing the risk of injury. When the benefits are real and begin to affect the nature of the game the ITF and USTA must review the rules of the game to maintain the desired nature of the sport. This is a complicated question that most sports face. More discussion, listening, research, and time are needed before the tennis community and governing bodies have the information necessary to shape the future of our game.

---

a mistiming of the impact point, the racquet speed and direction are still close to optimal.

If you are using a new, ultra-low mass tennis racquet, can you reduce your follow-through? The answer is no. The lower mass (inertia) of the racquet means that the arm may even have greater speed and kinetic energy after impact. The mass of the hand and arm segments are greater than the racquet, so it is always important for players to emphasize follow-through purely from an injury prevention perspective. However, the performance issues discussed above are also good reasons to emphasize good follow-throughs in groundstrokes.

SUMMARY AND MATCH POINTS

Forehand groundstroke techniques are strongly affected by the style of grip used by the player. The coordination used by the arm joints and strategic strengths and weakness are all associated with the different grips. A common

Stroke Technique Box

THE FOREHAND

The technique used by Roger Federer for a semi-open forehand is illustrated in Figure 4.11. A semi-open stance is about halfway between a square and an open stance. Federer's wide base of support sideward and forward give him a good compromise of stability and mobility (Balance and Inertia). The first image shows that he has used a large loop backswing. Also note that his rear leg is bent in a stretch-shortening cycle action that will vigorously drive the player's body and racquet upward. The racquet speed created by the loop backswing is then combined with the energy (Coordination and Transfer) generated by the primarily vertical leg drive. Players and coaches should not interpret these pictures to mean that Federer jumps then strokes, but that the vigorous rear leg drive and transfer of energy upward through the

body begins the movement. This allows the stroke to be initiated with the iner-tia of the ground and then only leaves the ground as a result of the upward drive off a stable base. A good leg drive forward (square stance) or more upward (open stance) is an important source of stroke power. The upward drive in a top-spin forehand should be separated from the common error of "pulling up" on the stroke. All players have made the coordination error of awkwardly pulling the trunk or racquet up prematurely. The good sequential coordination in Federer's arm action is apparent in the lag in the wrist just before impact in the next to last photo. Note that the upward motion of the body and racquet helps Federer cre-ate topspin on this forehand. It is almost impossible from this viewing angle and the small number of images to evaluate the speed and direction of this stroke. This Optimal Projection, the combination of speed, direction and spin, is impor-tant for coaches to evaluate in player's strokes. His follow-through is long and around the body.

Figure 4.11 *Semi-open stance forehand of Roger Federer. (Sequence images taken by Lance Jeffery and used with permission of USTA High Performance.)*

preparatory technique for all groundsrokes that improves mobility is the split step. The footwork, used to move to intercept the ball, however, varies with several effective techniques. There are a variety of effective stances for tennis forehands, ranging from open to closed. Each stance affects the coordination and transfer of energy that is used to drive the stroke, as well as subtle strengths and weaknesses. The forehand stroke typically involves some form of a loop backswing, forward swing, and a follow-through. The path of the racquet through impact and the angle and speed of the racquet face at impact are the most important factors in determining the speed and spin on the ball. The chapter outlined typical swing paths and racquet face angles that skilled players use for the topspin and backspin forehand.

Match Points

- Maximize the quickness of your preparation by timing your split step to your opponent's shot.

- A variety of footwork and stances are effective in the forehand.

- An open stance favors quick recovery over stroke speed and accuracy.

- A square stance favors stroke speed and accuracy over recovery after the stroke.

- At impact, most all forehands have the racquet face very close (less than 10 degrees) to vertical.

- Ball spin is primarily created by high-speed racquet motion along an angled path through the ball at impact.

- Flat forehands typically have upward racquet paths between 10 and 40 degrees at impact.

- Topspin forehands typically have upwared racquet paths between 35 and 50 degrees at impact.

- Backspin forehands typically have downwared (-10 to -40 degrees) racquet paths at impact.

Chapter Five

BIOMECHANICS
OF THE
BACKHAND

"Both the one-handed and two-handed backhand have specific characteristics that are conducive to optimal performance."— Jack Groppel

One of the continuing controversies in tennis relates to which is a better stroke, the one-handed or two-handed backhand? Groppel's quote above makes it clear that both can be highly-effective strokes. The quote also implies, correctly, that it is better to think about the strengths and weaknesses of each stroke rather than trying to define "best." Both backhand techniques have some similarities with the techniques of the forehand discussed in Chapter 4. Unfortunately, there has been less research on the backhand techniques than the forehand. This chapter will examine key backhand technique issues of grip, preparation and footwork, stance, stroke, and follow-through.

GRIPS

One-handed backhand. There are several grips used in one and two-handed backhands. One-handed backhands use either the eastern backhand or the continental grip. The full eastern backhand grip is the strongest, with the hand on top of the handle, a full quarter turn from the eastern forehand. The continental grip is weaker and requires small amounts of wrist flexion to square up the racquet face. Recall that in the forehand the grip strongly affects the forearm and wrist motions that can be used in the stroke. This is generally true of the backhands as well, but grip strength and racquet control are the more important issues in the one-handed backhand.

The eastern forehand grip cannot be recommended for the one-handed backhand. This grip requires considerable wrist flexion that weakens the grip muscles. Try this little experiment to illustrate the weakening of muscles when they are shortened considerably. Squeeze your opposite hand with your dominant hand and note the pressure on the opposite hand and the relatively straight or slightly extended gripping wrist. Now fully flex (bend the gripping wrist in the direction of the palm of your hand) about 70-90 degrees and now squeeze your opposite hand. The forearm muscles that contribute to a strong grip are considerably weakened because they are almost maximally shortened. The same loss of strength happens when tennis players use an incorrect grip in a one-handed backhand.

A one-handed backhand impacting the ball in a wrist-flexed position is a performance and injury disaster.

The situation is even worse when you look at the other wrist muscles. Muscles that are elongated also have less active force potential. The tension you feel in a stretching exercise is not strength but the passive tension of muscle and tendon being elongated. A one-handed backhand impacting the ball in a wrist-flexed position is a performance and injury disaster. In this situation, the wrist extensors are the main wrist muscle group supporting the weight of the racquet and resist the force of impact in the one-handed backhand (Figure 5.1). These muscles are weaker than the wrist flexors that provide the grip and wrist stability in the forehand, and to add to that, they are in a weakened, elongated position if the wrist is flexed. A beginner with a bent elbow and flexed-wrist one-handed backhand is creating a double overload of a weak muscle group. Long-term use of poor technique and inadequate rest will likely result in tennis elbow.

Two-handed backhand. Two-handed backhand grips influence both the strength and the coordination used in the stroke. Players usually add an eastern grip with the non-dominant hand to one of two grips for the dominant hand—the player's regular grip or one shifted toward a continental/backhand

The added strength in the forearms and grips in the two-handed backhand allows for later acceleration of the racquet and greater stability at impact.

Figure 5.1 *The wrist extensor muscles support the weight of the racquet and resist impact forces in the one-handed backhand. These muscles are weaker than the wrist flexors, and overuse of these muscles irritates the common attachment on the outside of the elbow (tennis elbow).*

grip. The addition of the non-dominant arm means that the impact point with the ball tends to be closer to the body, the trunk and arm actions tend to be more synchronized, and the added strength in the forearms and grips allows for later acceleration of the racquet and greater stability at impact.

PREPARATION AND FOOTWORK

In general, the consensus of the coaching wisdom is that preparation and footwork in the backhand may be slightly more important than in the forehand. In the one-handed backhand, the hitting shoulder is usually the front shoulder,

---

Advantage Box 5.1: Copying the Champ

Many young tennis players idolize a current champion and emulate his/her strokes. This occurs in all sports and can be a problem in tennis for several reasons. First, young players do not have the skill, strength, and basic technique of the elite player. Second, the signature shot or style of the latest champions is unique to them, and it may actually be a weakness for another player. Groppel (1992) notes that copying another player can be dangerous because you often do not know why that player strokes the way he does. One biomechanics textbook retold the story of a young athlete who worked diligently to emulate a technique point in a current Olympic champion. When the athlete finally qualfed for a competition with the champion and met him, he spoke of his admiration and struggle to master this technique. The young athlete was surprised to hear that he was emulating what the champion considered to be the major flaw in his technique that he was working hard to eliminate. It is also true that the tennis played at the elite level on the pro tour is very different from the tennis matches of beginning and recreational players. It is probably not a good idea for parents or coaches to squash a young player's natural admiration for an elite player's game, but it would be good to focus on the sound fundamentals in his game rather than idiosyncrasies. These fundamentals of tennis are consistent with the principles of biomechanics and will be there when the next interesting champion comes along.

---

so the impact point is more forward relative to the body, and there is little adaptability in this contact zone. In the forehand, the hitting shoulder is back and there are fewer adverse consequences in racquet alignment and speed if the ball is hit late. This is not true in the one-handed backhand, so it is vitally important that players use the split step and footwork discussed in Chapter 4 when setting up for one-handed backhands.

Two-handed backhands also may require extra attention to preparation and footwork because the contact zone tends to be closer to the body. The use of both arms that tend to be more bent than in many forehands, requires that player positions himself carefully to be able to intercept the ball closer to his body than for a one-handed backhand or forehand.

STANCES

As in the forehand, the stance used in the backhand also affects how weight transfers and what body actions can contribute to racquet speed (Coordination and Transfer). Backhands can be hit from semi-open stances to a closed stance. One-handed backhands should most often be hit from a square stance to maximize the use of the linear motion of the body. One-handed backhands, with the hitting shoulder toward the ball, tend to have less trunk rotation available to generate racquet speed than in a forehand. Semi-open backhands are not usually recommended because this also limits the ability to use trunk rotation to help generate racquet speed. Two-handed backhands have slightly more flexibility in the hitting zone because there are two arms to generate racquet speed, so use of weaker stances might not be a problem.

STROKE

One-handed backhands. One-handed backhands have similar loop backswings as forehands. The forward swing through impact for various spins also follows similar trajectories as reported for the forehand in Chapter 4. The arm joint motions used in the one-handed backhand are different than in the forehand, this has profound implications on how players apply the principles of Coordination and Transfer of Energy and Range of Motion in their backhands.

Many of the arm motions to create a one-handed backhand occur at the shoulder. Key motions are horizontal abduction (drawing the arm from the opposite hip "pocket" around the body) and external rotation (a long axis rotation of the whole right arm to the right). Other key joint actions are elbow extension, forearm supination (forearm equivalent of external rotation), and wrist extension (moving toward the back of the hand). Skilled players tend to contact the ball with the wrist hyperextended (Figure 5.2). Hyperextension occurs when the wrist is rotated toward the back of the hand past neutral. This wrist position is a stronger impact position than the more wrist-flexed position common in less skilled players (Blackwell and Cole, 1994; Knudson and Blackwell, 1997). Recall the little exercise on gripping your opposite hand. It turns out that the wrist position where the grip is strongest is in slight wrist hyperextension. Skilled players holding the racquet head up with wrist hyperextension at

The added strength in the forearms and grips in the two-handed backhand allows for later acceleration of the racquet and greater stability at impact.

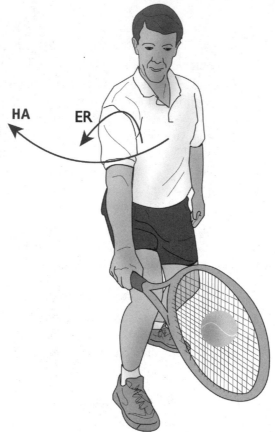

Figure 5.2 *At impact in the one-handed backhand, the wrist is hyperextended. This is a strong grip position which helps transfer energy from the hand and arm to the racquet and provides resistance to the shock wave after impact. Key arm motions that create the backhand are shoulder horizontal abduction (HA) and external rotation (ER).*

impact in the one-handed backhand have more resistance and range of motion in which to absorb the shock wave of impact.

In summary, the one-handed backhand may appear be more dependent on shoulder motion than the forehand, but it would be a mistake to discount the importance of the motions (and stability) of the elbow, wrist, and hand. The lesser amount of trunk rotation in the backhand relative to the forehand also argues for the effective integration of a weight shift to transfer energy quickly through the trunk to the racquet arm.

The advantages of a one-handed backhand over a two-handed backhand are flexibility in adjusting to a wide variety of ball bounces, creation of a variety of ball spins, and greater reach away from the body. The disadvantages are the demands the one-handed technique places on the wrist extensors and the coordination of more arm actions to create racquet speed.

Two-handed backhands. The two-handed backhand stroke is slightly different than a one-handed backhand or a nondominant forehand. While the racquet backswing follows a looped path similar to forehands, the range of motion is reduced because both arms are used and tend to be slightly bent. There has been some controversy as to the general coordination and use of body motions used to create the two-handed forward stroke.

Jack Groppel's early studies of the one and two-handed backhand led him to the conclusion that the two-handed stroke was primarily created by two key motions (Groppel, 1992). He hypothesized that the two-handed technique consisted of lower body action and an integrated trunk and arm action. A skilled two-handed backhand would then essentially be a weight shift with hip rotation, followed by trunk rotation with the arms and racquet rotating with the trunk (Figure 5.3). A recent study has reported greater trunk motion and lower back torques in the two-handed backhand compared to the one-handed backhand (Kawasaki, et al. 2005). Groppel also suggested that players minimize wrist motion during the stroke. This suggestion was very similar to the classic tennis instruction emphasizing a leg drive and trunk/shoulder centered groundstrokes, with a firm grip that minimizes wrist action.

A recent study comparing one- and two-handed backhands, however, is more consistent with other groundstroke studies that report a variety of joint motions that contribute to racquet speed (Reid and Elliott, 2001). These authors studied skilled college players and found that there was no difference in racquet speed at impact between backhand techniques and that both backhands essentially used five major body segment actions (hips, shoulders,

 **In a recent study of college players, there was no difference in racquet speed at impact between backhand techniques and both backhands used five major body segment actions (hips, shoulders, upper arm, forearm, wrists/hands).**

Figure 5.3 *One coordination strategy of a two-handed backhand essentially uses two sources of energy to accelerate the racquet—(1) leg/hip action and (2) trunk/arm action (Groppel, 1992).*

upper arm, forearm, wrists/hands). This coordination is illustrated in Figure 5.4. The improved three-dimensional experimental technique in this study and its consistency with the variety of coordination combinations seen in other groundstrokes leads me to the conclusion that two-handed backhands also use a variety of arm actions to create racquet speed. The belief that the two-handed backhand has to be easier to coordinate than a one-handed backhand may not be true. It is also possible that the recent strategy of offensive, high-speed groundstrokes might mean that more and more players with two-handed backhands will be using more sequential, multi-segment coordination.

Figure 5.4 *The more multi-segment coordination in the two-handed backhand observed in a recent study (Reid and Elliott, 2001). This technique may be more common in modern players.*

One observation in the Reid and Elliott (2001) study related to disguise was not controversial, but it was important experimental verification of coaching wisdom. The study examined shot direction and spin and found evidence of a delayed acceleration of the racquet toward the target in the two-handed backhands relative to one-handed backhands. This verified the belief that skilled players with two-handed backhands can more quickly adjust the racquet closer to impact to disguise shot speed and direction than can one-handed players.

Integration Box 5.1

One or Two-Handed?

A common backhand technique question is whether there is an overriding advantage of a one- or two-handed backhand. Biomechanical data can provide some information on this topic but, again, this must be integrated with other relevant factors. Strategic issues related to the sport, opponents, injury, surfaces, and the individual player all must be weighed with any biomechanical differences between the strokes. Currently, the data support the conclusion that both backhand techniques can be equally effective, so coaches and players should let player preference and other strategic factors guide their decisions about preferred backhand technique. This fact alone is a good illustration of our previous discussion that there is no one perfect or best stroke. Some beginners might find a two-handed backhand easier to use because of the extra strength of the second hand or a preference for a more compact, simultaneous stroking action that is easier to coordinate. Some players might find that the one-handed backhand feels more natural and easier. It makes little sense to ask a player comfortable with long, flowing one-handed strokes to consider a quicker, bent-arm two-handed backhand. Only a lack of success with biomechanical errors using a backhand technique along with other player factors (e.g., strength, strategic, psychological) would be a good indicator to try the opposite backhand technique.

FOLLOW-THROUGH

The nature of the follow-through in the backhand very much depends on the ball spin created and if the player is using a one or a two-handed grip. There is virtually no systematic comparative research on the variety of follow-throughs used in tennis. Each of the ones described is effective. Players should strive to elongate and gradually slow the racquet using the follow-through that feels most natural to them.

One-handed topspin backhands tend to finish with the racquet high above the head. One-handed backspin strokes have a loop-like pattern where the racquet continues downward after impact but gradually begins to loop back up to easily transition to a ready position.

The two-handed backhand has a wide variety of follow-through patterns. These follow-throughs fall into two groups depending on whether the non-dominant hand is dropped from the handle. Players who prefer to keep both

Figure 5.5 *The follow-through of a two-handed backhand often wraps around the player's body.*

 The nature of the follow-through in the backhand very much depends on the ball spin created and if the player is using a one or a two-handed grip.

Stroke Technique Box

THE TWO-HANDED BACKHAND

The technique used by Nicolas Kiefer in an defensive two-handed backhand is illustrated in the Figure 5.6. It is comforting for regular players to see that the pros are human and are forced to hit awkward strokes. It's not so comforting to know that we would not survive the time and motion pressure of one professional stroke, much less the barrage of great shots that constitutes a professional rally. How do we know that this two-handed backhand was not a typical stroke for Kiefer? Note that Kiefer is well behind the baseline, jammed close to his body, and hitting from a semi-open stance. Most two-handed backhand are hit from square or slightly closed stances. Kiefer makes the best of a tough situation by strong extension of the rear leg to drive his backhand. Because there is little time, the loop of the backswing is very small. The coordination used in this two-handed backhand resembles the traditional two-handed with only a few body actions (Coordination and Transfer). Following the leg drive, Kiefer's forward swing is primarily from trunk rotation with limited arm and wrist action. Also notice that there is only a slightly upward racquet path through impact so the ball spin will tend to be flat or with minimal topspin. Kiefer's follow-through is upward and around his head. Coaches need to remember that defensive or emergency strokes do not need to have perfect technique. When observing and evaluating technique, the coach should watch several strokes to identify patterns of stroking weaknesses and strengths. Kiefer has an excellent two-handed backhand and effectively uses a variety stances and coordination of the legs and upper body.

Figure 5.6 *A two-handed backhand by Nicolas Kiefer. (Sequence images taken by Lance Jeffery and used with permission of USTA High Performance.)*

Stroke Technique Box

THE ONE-HANDED BACKHAND

The technique used by Justine Henin-Hardenne in an one-handed backhand is illustrated in Figure 5.7. Notice the early racquet preparation in a small loop and wide closed stance used in this backhand. This stance provides a wide, stable base of support on which to hit the stroke, but notice how the left hip limits the hip rotation. Using a closed stance to emphasize stability in an aggressive backhand is a perfect choice for this shot from the middle of the court. Henin-Hardenne's excellent footwork and racquet preparation allow for a large Range of Motion to be used to create racquet speed at impact. Notice the extension of the arm away from the body at impact (photo 3) and the wrist hyperextension at impact. The low-to-high racquet path creates topspin on the ball. The very high and across the body follow-through ensures that this long, flowing stroke creates great ball speed and spin. The coordination that transfers energy in this stroke is extension of the legs, trunk twist, and shoulder horizontal abduction and external rotation. This is a beautifully coordinated stroke. Opponents probably often wondered how such a small woman (low inertia) could hit such a "heavy" ball on her one-handed backhand.

Figure 5.7 *The classic one-handed backhand by Justine Henin-Hardenne. (Sequence images taken by Lance Jeffery and used with permission of USTA High Performance.)*

hands on the racquet tend to have more trunk rotation in the follow-through, and either wrap the racquet and arms overhead or around the body (Figure 5.5). Most players who release the non-dominant hand tend to wrap the racquet overhead, but can also swing the racquet to the opposite side of the body.

SUMMARY AND MATCH POINTS

The one-handed and two-handed backhands seem to be equally effective strokes. There are advantages and disadvantages to each that should be considered by players and coaches when learning the stroke or thinking about a change in technique. Racquet speed in one-handed backhands is primarily created by a weight shift and two major shoulder joint motions. The wrist extensors are used in the one-handed backhand to hold up the racquet and resist the force of impact but are not usually used to speed up the racquet because they are weaker than the wrist flexors.

The two-handed backhand can be hit with minimal sequential coordination (two body actions) or more body segments. The two-handed backhand does appear to have an advantage in being able to accelerate the racquet very close to impact, potentially increasing the player's ability to disguise shot direction. These biomechanical factors should be weighed with individual, strategic, and other factors when making decisions about backhand technique.

Match Points

- Both one-handed and two-handed backhands are effective, but have strengths and weaknesses.

- One-handed backhands create racquet speed primarily with weight shift and two shoulder movements.
  -Strengths are flexibility in impact position, a long flowing stroke, and a variety of spins.
  -Weaknesses are wrist extensor strength demands and fewer body motions to accelerate the racquet..

- Two-handed backhand create racquet speed with a variety of body segment coordination patterns.
  -Strengths are decreased stress on the arms and ability to disguise shot direction.
  -Weaknesses are footwork demands for restricted reach and backspin generation.

Chapter Six

BIOMECHANICS
OF THE
VOLLEY

"...most volleys are control shots." – Dennis Van Der Meer

A tennis player in the forecourt preparing to volley is on the offensive and looking to end the point. A volley that intercepts the ball in flight a couple feet from the net clearly emphasizes shot accuracy and control over speed. The short amount of time available (often less than half a second) to execute this shot adds to the accuracy demands of the volley, so volleys require good preparation, anticipation, precision, and quickness. In addition, there is less need for racquet head speed than in a groundstroke because the ball has not slowed down much by the time a player intercepts it, so it will naturally rebound at a higher speed. Additionally, the ball will travel a shorter distance back to the opponent's backcourt, thereby decreasing his time to respond.

The optimal techniques for the volley, a stroke that emphasizes accuracy over speed, are different than the techniques used in the groundstrokes (where racquet speed is important). Volley techniques are consistent with the principles of Range of Motion and Optimal Projection. Unique aspects of forehand versus backhand volley, grips, preparation/footwork, stroke, and follow-through will be discussed.

GRIPS

A controversial area in volley technique is whether to switch between a forehand and backhand grip or to use a continental grip for both forehand and backhand volleys. Unfortunately, this is an area where biomechanics research has not been conducted, so we only have indirect evidence of what subjects in some studies normally do. Fortunately, there are areas (groundstrokes and service returns) where both techniques have been commonly observed to be effective in skilled players, so players need only know the trade-offs and decide which technique is better for themselves.

The advantages of switching between grips are greater stability and ease of squaring the racquet face to the ball. Naturally, the disadvantage is that it takes some time to change grips, and advanced players often angle the racquet face to create backspin on most of their volleys.

The advantages of using only a continental grip are the simplicity of not changing grips and a slight angle on the racquet face that contributes to ball spin. The disadvantages of the continental grip are the weaker grip and the need to make other small rotations in arm joints to orient the racquet face. For example, forehand down-the-line volleys using a continental grip are more difficult because the grip tends to angle the racquet face to the left. Extra wrist extension or other elbow and shoulder motions are needed to point the racquet more to the near sideline.

Which grip is best for a particular player clearly depends on many factors. Beginners are often taught to change grips, presumably because the change is an important skill they are working on, their grips tend to be weaker, and they would most likely benefit from easily creating a square racquet face to the ball. Advanced players often use a continental grip because their grip is stronger, play is faster, they want to create spin on their volleys, and they are more skilled at making minute adjustments of the arm joints during a volley.

PREPARATION AND FOOTWORK

As with groundstrokes, the volley movement is set up by a good split step and footwork to intercept the ball. Research on skilled players shows that there are two major types of footwork in hitting a volley, a side step (open stance) volley and a cross-over step (square/closed stance). The tendency is for the majority of the volleys to be cross-over step shots because this moves the player closer to the net (better angles on the shot) and increases the speed of the volley (Figure 6.1). Open stance volleys tend to occur more often in close or high-speed (reflex) volleys (Chow et al. 1999). Because there is no specific tennis research comparing the specific footwork techniques, players and coaches can only be guided by general theory. In theory, the cross-over step is preferred for

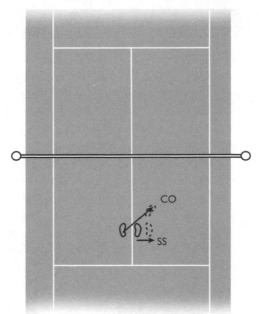

Figure 6.1 *Cross-over footwork in the volley is preferred over a side step because the player can move farther forward and sideward. This increases the speed of the volley and the angles (sideward and downward) at which the ball can be hit into the court.*

most volleys. The extra forward and sideward motion in pushing off the nearer foot in the cross-over step and positioning for additional steps appear to be clear advantages over the side step (open stance) volley. The cross-over footwork helps contribute to the forward and downward motion of the racquet that creates good ball speed and backspin.

STROKE

The volley tends to be a simpler and shorter stroke than the groundstrokes. This is consistent with the speed-accuracy trade-off and the principle of Range of Motion. The decrease in the number of body segments and range of motion used helps reduce the complexity of the movement, increasing the potential accuracy. In tennis instruction this is expressed by saying that the volley backswing and forward swing should be short, so the stroke looks like a "punch" or "block" of the racquet. The key idea conveyed by these cues is that the volley is a short stroke, not that there is complete extension of the arm joints to hit the ball. Observation of advanced players shows this general impression is true, and these are likely good images to use, but the research also shows that there is really a range of body-segment motions in volley techniques.

Advantage Box 6.1: Vision and Reacion Time

Notice that you are nearing the end of this book and there has been nothing written about watching the ball. The time pressures of hitting volleys puts a premium on good anticipation, vision, and reaction to intercept the ball. In this last advantage box we will explore several surprising facts about how tennis players use their eyes to predict ball flight and bounce. The first and most important issue is that the eyes use a variety of movements and are naturally good at tracking moving objects like the ball. Stand a meter apart from your playing partner and ask him to catch in one hand a tennis ball that you toss in a soft, underhand motion. After a few trials ask him to close his eyes and still catch the ball, where you say "close" just after you release the ball. You will find that virtually all people (especially tennis players) will be able to catch most tosses and will almost always be able to move their hand to intercept the ball's trajectory. Studies of eye motion in tennis players has shown that the important time to focus visual attention on the ball is during its initial trajectory or as it is being hit. Cues like "keep your eye on the ball" or watch it "hit your racquet" are miscues. Tennis players use fast eye movements (saccades) that jump from one fixation point on the ball to another in its trajectory. Players cannot smoothly roll both their eyes along with the whole path of the ball as it travels toward you. Next time you see some sport action photography of tennis or other striking sports, notice that the athlete's eyes are usually focused at the last fixation ahead of the ball impact point.

Coaches need to encourage players to focus visual attention on their opponent and the ball in a rally. This ensures good visual attention to the initial trajectory of the ball, and it may foster the development of shot anticipation skills. Considerable research has been conducted in this area as to what skilled players look at when the opponent is hitting and if these visual skills can be trained. Research has shown that skilled players do have different visual search patterns that differ from beginning players. Beginners tend to look all over an opponent, and their eyes are often focused on the opponent's racquet. A fairly consistent trend in the research is that skilled players tend to have focused visual targets that match the opponent's stroke, in that the eyes focus more on trunk, arm action, and then the ball. Good visual anticipation skills can ensure that a player is mimizing reaction time and allowing more time to move and execute strokes. Readers interested in this research are encouraged to begin their study with three recent papers (Farrow and Abernethy, 2002; Shim et al. 2005; Williams et al. 2002).

When reacting to a visual stimulus like the flight of a ball, athletes can react quickly, but the speed of reaction depends on the complexity of the possible responses. A tennis split-step in the forecourt presents a very complex situation, much more difficult than springing out of the blocks in a sprint. Typical reaction times of adult tennis players to initiate movement toward a volley are between 200 and 250 ms (1/5 to 1/4 second). About half of this time is taken up in seeing the ball, processing the information, and selecting the best movement response. If you only have a half a second to react and intercept a fast groundstroke at the net, you can see that it is important for players to practice split-steps, early visual focus on the opponent and ball, and quick movement to intercept the ball for successful volleys.

The traditional volley with the smallest range of motion is commonly called the "punch" volley, while a more vigorous volley from a position near the service line is called a "drive" volley (Groppel, 1992). These volleys all are sufficiently different from groundstrokes in that they use less range of motion and fewer body segment motions to maximize stroke accuracy. Integration Box 6.1 highlights the very recent trend of players actually playing "swing" or groundstroke-like volleys.

PUNCH VOLLEY

Research does show that racquet motion in the volley has a more direct path (Van Gheluwe and Hebbelinck, 1986) and uses a more simultaneous coordination of the stroke (Elliott et al. 1988; Wang et al. 2002) than groundstrokes. Figure 6.2 illustrates the typical paths of the racquet head in a forehand volley and forehand groundstroke.

Elliott et al. (1988), however, found that skilled players used more range of motion than was commonly advocated by coaching literature. Most skilled

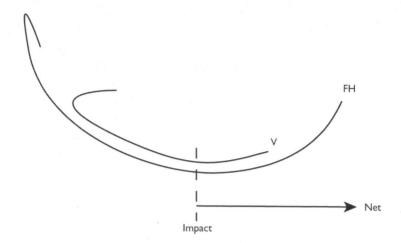

Figure 6.2 *Top view of typical racquet paths in a forehand volley and groundstroke. Note the shorter range of motion and more direct path of the volley relative to the groundstroke.*

players clearly took the racquet back past the rear shoulder in preparing to volley. The backswing for a volley was a short, upwards and backwards motion that was synchronized with body turn and motion to intercept the ball. Racquet preparation for the forehand volleys tended to keep the racquet nearly pointing upward, while in the backhand, the racquet tended to lag farther back.

Skilled players created a quick and controlled downward and forward racquet motion to the ball, with some elbow and wrist motion to speed up the racquet. This is in conflict with typical coaching literature that suggests that there be virtually no wrist motion in the volley, and it also indicates that some players may use small elements of sequential coordination in some volleys. The study did confirm coaching opinions that the ball is impacted just ahead of the body. The path of the racquet through impact in forehand and backhand volleys is slightly downward, and this, combined with a slightly open racquet face, creates a fast shot with backspin.

Skilled players use only a slightly abbreviated follow-through because the racquet can retain 75 to 95 percent of the pre-impact speed. Two racquet motions are typically observed. One is a gradual continuation of the forward and downward motion, and the other is a more abrupt slowing and opening of the racquet face. This latter follow-thorough, which has been called a "dishing" effect, then, like the other follow-through, continues to bring the racquet back to the ready position. Recall that in Chapter 2 we noted that very-high speed imaging of all tennis strokes shows a violent shock wave that slows the forward motion of the racquet momentarily.

Extreme or adverse slowing and twisting of the racquet face is usually symptomatic of an off-center impact, slower racquet speed, or a weak grip. The mechanical significance of this "dished" follow-through can be quite variable. A volley with low racquet speed and impacted off-center on the racquet face will usually not be hit very well. Another volley that is hit with good racquet speed, using a moderate grip and is hit slightly off-center might look the same in the follow-through but the ball can be hit quite well. Downward deflection or "dishing" of a volley can be expected given the backspin on most volleys and should not be considered direct evidence of a bad volley. A pattern of weak volleys with exaggerated "dishing" of the racquet should be a warning to players and coaches that there are weaknesses in the grip strength, racquet speed development, or the intercepting of the ball using the middle of the racquet face.

Skilled players clearly use a smaller the range of motion and more simultaneous coordination in the "punch" volley than in groundstrokes.

As was mentioned earlier in the groundstrokes, side-to-side directional control in the volley appears to be a matter of timing. Down-the-line volleys have the racquet head at or behind the wrist, while cross-court volleys tend to occur more forward with the racquet just ahead of the wrist (Figure 6.3).

Skilled players clearly use a smaller the range of motion and more simultaneous coordination in the "punch" volley than in groundstrokes. Research shows that these trends are not as pronounced as some common teaching cues, but the overcompensation in these cues might be messages that help many players create different coordination in their volleys. We will see that there is slightly more motion used in the "drive" volley and, therefore, a greater potential for expert agreement about whether the motion of any joint can be described as restricted or free.

(a)   **(b)**

Figure 6.3 Directional control of a volley is determined primarily by orientation of the racquet face. A cross-court volley tends to be impacted ahead of the wrist (a), while a down-the-line volley tends to be hit above or behind the wrist (b).

Integration Box 6.1
Recent Technique Changes—The Swing Volley

The relatively recent strategic emphasis of high-speed, offensive shots from all over the court has influenced volley technique. Many players now perform a "swing volley" rather than a punch or a drive volley. This volley may even have topspin rather than the backspin of "punch" and "drive" volleys. It is my opinion that is swing volley is chosen not because of its tactical superiority to a traditional volley but for its psychological and show-business aspects. There probably has not been any systematic study comparing the error and success rates of these two volleys, but many modern players simply choose to go with a more familiar hit all-out strategy despite a higher likelihood of errors than a traditional drive volley. Modern players have not improved their court coverage to the extent that racquet power has improved. A player has to decide if the greater risk of hitting the ball out or into the tape is worth the in-your-face showmanship of tying to smack the ball through your opponent. This is a technique that should clearly not be emulated by recreational tennis players.

DRIVE VOLLEY

Elliott et al. (1988) also studied the "drive" volley and found only slightly higher racquet speeds than the "punch" volley. They also found that most arm joints have greater range of motion at the end of preparation, so that the racquet was 30 to 50 percent farther behind the back shoulder in a service line volley than a net volley.

The greater range of motion used in a "drive" volley tends to decrease the potential accuracy of the shot. This very consistent observation in many sports has also been observed in the tennis volley. Groppel (1992) qualitatively described the results of a film study of the "drive" and "punch" volley using players of various abilities. Only advanced players were effective at hitting "drive" volleys based on the criteria of consistent central impacts on the racquet and ball speed. Beginner and intermediate subjects had difficulty in using the larger range of motion in a "drive" volley, but all levels of players had greater accuracy in using the "punch" volley technique (Figure 6.4).

More research is clearly needed on the various volley techniques. It is likely that the greater range of motion in a drive volley increases the speed of the ball, but only if the ball is cleanly impacted on the racquet face. Studies have to be carefully designed to control for impact conditions (height, ball speed, spin,

Figure 6.4 *A less skilled player using the larger range of motion of a "drive" or swing volley may not hit the ball faster if they lack the control to precisely intercept the ball (speed and impact location on the racquet face).*

etc.) and other variables to answer these basic questions about the extent of the trade-offs between "drive" and "punch" volleys. These kinds of studies must then be combined with research in real tennis play conditions, as well as other strategic information for coaches and players to know what volley techniques are the most effective.

Volleys are like groundstrokes in that racquet speed and a central impact on the racquet face are key to a high-speed shot. Players who add more range of motion or segment motions to increase racquet speed will likely volley faster, but at a cost of diminishing accuracy.

Volleys are like groundstrokes in that racquet speed and a central impact on the racquet face are key to a high-speed shot. Players who add more range of motion or segment motions to increase racquet speed will likely volley faster, but at a cost of diminishing accuracy. Occasionally, a player will attempt a drop volley to an open spot on the court because the opponent is completely out of position. A drop volley strives to minimize ball speed so the ball bounces near the net, so the racquet must be slowed down prior to impact. Groppel (1992) decribes this well and notes that the teaching that a player should make sudden drops of the racquet or grip pressure at impact are probably not good cues. A recent study has reported relatively minor differences in joint motions between a regular and a drop volley (Wang et al. 2002). Drop volleys or short angled volleys are executed by slowing the racquet up to the impact position, rather than the usual increase in racquet speed up to impact.

OPTIMAL PROJECTION

One of the greatest advantages of hitting volleys is the increased margin for error in the shot. The proximity to the net dramatically increases the side-to-side angles available to the player, and if the ball is intercepted above the level of the net, the vertical angles available are also much larger than in groundstrokes. These accuracy advantages combined with the greater temporal and psychological pressure on the opponent to hit difficult passing shots or lobs makes the volley a very important offensive shot.

The window or margin for vertical error in a typical flat groundstroke from the baseline is about 10 degrees. When the player moves into a volleying position 3 feet from the net, the vertical margin for error increases to well over 20

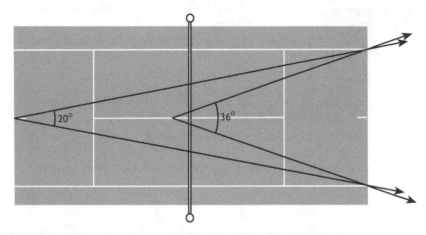

Figure 6.5 *The range of possible horizontal angles at groundstroke and volleying positions shows a larger margin for error in the volley.*

degrees (Brody, 1987). The baseliner at the center mark has a horizontal window of successful angles of about 20 degrees (10 to right or left) to the corners from the geometry of the court (Figure 6.5). At a volleying position, this horizontal window of success is now about 36 degrees. In reality, the skilled player can combine a sideward and downward angle into the forecourt, especially when closer to the net, so windows of success over 100 degrees are possible.

One of the greatest advantages of hitting volleys is the increased margin for error in the shot. The proximity to the net dramatically increases the side-to-side angles available to the player, and if the ball is intercepted above the level of the net, the vertical angles available are also much larger than in groundstrokes.

SUMMARY AND MATCH POINTS

One of the most important offensive strokes in tennis is the volley because it has a larger margin for error than groundstrokes. The temporal and strategic demands of volleys, however, require a shorter stroke technique than groundstrokes. Classic "punch" and "drive" volleys tend to use more simultaneous motions of the legs, trunk, and racquet arm than the sequential movements of

Stroke Technique Box

THE VOLLEY

The technique used by Pete Sampras in a high volley is illustrated in Figure 6.6. In photo 1 Sampras is springing out of the split step to move forward and to the side for the forehand volley. Notice the short shoulder horizontal abduction used in backswing (photo 2). The forward push of the volley is a short, controlled use of the Range of Motion of the shoulder and elbow joints. Sampras creates controlled racquet speed by moving forward in a nearly square stance and impacts the ball with a comfortably extended arm. The slightly downward racquet path through the ball creates backspin on the ball and optimized the angle of ball flight to the target cross-court. Two aspects of his follow-through are important. First, it is short because high racquet speed was not needed, and second the racquet head stayed high. A racquet head that stays up and does not get deflected a long distance downward usually indicates the player has good muscular stabilization of the wrist and arm. Notice how a short and more simultaneous body motion is used in this volley. Sampras impacts the ball accurately, right on the sweetspot of the strings. He is also able to use the speed of the return with this firm volley to hit an aggressive cross-court volley from the service line. Most players who are temped to hit a swing volley in these situations are making a poor trade-off by losing accuracy when the racquet speed does not have to be great.

Figure 6.6 *A high forehand volley by Pete Sampras. (Sequence images taken by Lance Jeffery and used with permission of USTA High Performance.)*

the groundstrokes. The movement is not strictly simultaneous because advanced players do use slightly more range of motion and more joint motions to create racquet speed. Players who use full-swing volleys are using a technique mismatched to the demands of the game.

Match Points

- Effective volleys may be hit with a continental grip and by switching between eastern and backhand grips for forehand and backhand volleys.

- Footwork to move an intercept a volley from a split-step should usually be a cross-over step.

- To maximize accuracy, volley technique tends to use less range of motion and more simultaneous coordination than groundstrokes.

- The offensive court position for most volleys creates larger and wider angles into the court, so there is a greater margin for error than groundstrokes.

- The forward stroke in most volleys is slightly downward to create backspin.

- Recent volleys with larger ranges of motion (drive and swing volleys) are risky shots because accuracy is reduced and greater ball speed could be lost by an off-center impact on the racquet face.

REFERENCES

Andrew, D.P.S., Chow, J.W., Knudson, D.V., & Tillman, M.D. (2003). Effect of ball size on player reaction and racket acceleration during the tennis volley. Journal of Science and Medicine in Sport, 6, 102-112.

Ariel, G.B., & Braden, V. (1979). Biomechanical analysis of ballistic vs. tracking movements in tennis skills. In J. Groppel (Ed). Proceedings of a National Symposium on the Racquet Sports (pp. 105-124). Champaign, IL: University of Illinois.

Baechle, T.R., & Earle, R.W. (Eds). (2000). Essentials of Strength Training and Conditioning 2nd ed. Champaign, IL: Human Kinetics.

Bahamonde, R. (2005). Biomechanics of the elbow joint during tennis strokes. International SportMed Journal, 6(2), 42-63.

Bahamonde, R. (2000). Changes in angular momentum during the tennis serve. Journal of Sports Sciences, 18, 579-592.

Bahamonde, R., & Knudson, D. (2003). Linear and angular momentum in stroke production. In: B. Elliott, M. Reid, & M. Crespo (Eds). Biomechanics of Advanced Tennis Coaching. (pp. 49-70). London: International Tennis Federation.

Bisset, L., Paungmali, A., Vicenzino, B., & Beller, E. (2005). A systematic review and meta-analysis of clinical trials on physical interventions for lateral epicondylalgia. British Journal of Sports Medicine, 39, 411-422.

Blackwell, J., & Cole, K. (1994). Wrist kinematics differ in expert and novice tennis players performing the backhand stroke: implications for tennis elbow. Journal of Biomechanics, 27, 509-516.

Blackwell, J., & Knudson, D. (2005). Vertical plane margins for error in the topspin forehand of intermediate tennis players. Medicina Sportiva, 9(3), 40-43.

Blackwell, J., & Knudson, D. (2002). Effect of the type 3 (oversize) tennis ball on serve performance and upper extremity muscle activity. Sports Biomechanics, 1, 187-192.

Blievernicht, J. (1968). Accuracy in the tennis forehand drive: a cinematographic analysis. Research Quarterly, 39, 776-779.

Bower, R., & Cross, R. (2005). String tension effects on tennis ball rebound speed and accuracy during playing conditions. Journal of Sports Sciences, 23, 765-771.

Bragg, R.W., & Andriacchi, T.P. (2001). The lateral reaction step in tennis footwork. In J. Blackwell (Ed). Proceedings of Poster Sessions: XIX International Symposium on Biomechanics in Sports (pp. 34-37). San Francisco: University of San Francisco.

Brody, H. (1987). Tennis Science for Tennis Players. Philadelphia, PA: University of Pennsylvania Press.

Brody, H., Cross, R., & Lindsey, C. (2002). The Physics and Technology of Tennis. Solana Beach, CA: Racquet Tech Publishing.

References

Chandler, T.J., Ellenbecker, T., & Roetert, P. (1998). Sport-specific muscle strength imbalances in tennis. Strength and Conditioning, 20(2), 7-10.

Chen, G. (2006). Induced acceleration contributions to locomotion dynamics are not physically well defined. Gait and Posture, 23, 37-44.

Chow, J.W., Carlton, L.G., Chae, W., Shim, J., Lim, Y., & Kuenster, A. (1999). Movement characteristics of the tennis volley. Medicine and Science in Sports and Exercise, 31, 855-863.

Chow, J.W., Carlton, L.G., Lim, Y., Chae, W., Shim, J., Kuenster, A., & Kokubun, K. (2003). Comparing the pre- and post-impact ball and racquet kinematics of elite tennis players' first and second serves: a preliminary study. Journal of Sports Sciences, 21, 529-537.

Chow, J., Knudson, D., & Tillman, M. D. (submitted). Muscle activation during the volley with the regular and oversize tennis ball.

Chu, D. (1995). Power Tennis Training. Champaign, IL: Human Kinetics.

Cooke, A. et al. (2003). The Science of Tennis [CD-ROM]. London: Sport Science and Engineering in Education.

Coutinho, C., Pezarat-Correia, P., & Veloso, A. (2004). EMG patterns of the upper limb muscles in the first (flat) and second (topspin) serve performed by a top player. Medicine and Science in Tennis, 9(4), 14-15.

Cross, R. (2005). Bounce of a spinning tennis ball near normal incidence. American Journal of Physics, 73, 914-920.

Cross, R. (2002). Ball spin and bounce off the court. In: Brody, H. Cross, R., & Lindsey, C. The Physics and Technology of Tennis (pp. 343-357). Solana Beach, CA: Racquet Tech Publishing.

Dignall, R.J., Goodwill, S.R., & Haake, S.J. (2004). Tennis GUT-Modeling the game. In M. Hubbard, R.D. Mehta, & J.M. Pallis (Eds.) The Engineering of Sport 5: Volume 2 (pp. 382-388). Sheffield: International Sports Engineering Association.

Dixon, S.J., & Stiles, V.H. (2003). Impact absorption of tennis shoe-surface combinations. Sports Engineering, 6, 1-10.

Elliott, B. (1988). Biomechanics of the serve in tennis: a biomedical perspective. Sports Medicine, 6, 285-294.

Elliott, B. (1983). Spin and the power serve in tennis. Journal of Human Movement Studies, 9, 97-104.

Elliott, B., & Christmass, M. (1995). A comparison of the high and low backspin backhand drives in tennis using different grips. Journal of Sports Sciences, 13, 141-151.

Elliott, B., Fleisig, G., Nicholls, R., & Escamilla, R. (2003). Technique effects on upper limb loading in the tennis serve. Journal of Science and Medicine in Sport, 6, 76-87.

Elliott, B., Marshall, R., & Noffal, G. (1995). Contributions of upper limb segment rotations during the power serve in tennis. Journal of Applied Biomechanics, 11, 433-442.

Elliott, B., & Marsh, T. (1989). A biomechanical comparison of the topspin and back-spin forehand approach shots in tennis. Journal of Sports Sciences, 7, 215-227.

Elliott, B., Marsh, T., & Overheu, P. (1989a). A biomechanical comparison of the multisegment and single unit topspin forehand drives in tennis. International Journal of Sport Biomechanics, 5, 350-364.

Elliott, B., Marsh, T., & Overheu, P. (1989b). The topspin backhand drive in tennis: a biomechanical analysis. Journal of Human Movement Studies, 16, 1-16.

Elliott, B., Overheu, P., & Marsh, A.P. (1988). The service line and net volley in tennis: a cinematographic analysis. Australian Journal of Science and Medicine in Sport, 20(2), 10-18.

Elliott, B., Reid, M., & Crespo, M. (Eds). (2003).Biomechanics of Advanced Tennis. London: International Tennis Federation.

Elliott, B., & Wood, G. (1983). The biomechanics of the foot-up and foot-back tennis service techniques. Australian Journal of Sport Science, 3(2), 3-6.

Farrow, D., & Abernethy, B. (2002). Can anticipatory skills be learned through implicit video-based perceptual training. Journal of Sports Sciences, 20, 471-485.

Fleisig, G., Nicholls, R., Elliott, B., & Escamilla, R. (2003). Kinematics used by world class tennis players to produce high-velocity serves. Sports Biomechanics, 2, 51-71.

Gerritsen, K.G.M., Nigg, B.M., & Wright, I.M. (2002). Shoes and surfaces in tennis: injury and performance aspects. In: P. Renstrom (Ed). Handbook of Sports Medicine and Science: Tennis (pp 39-45). Oxford: Blackwell Science.

Girard, O., Micallef, J., & Millet, G.P. (2005). Lower-limb activity during the power serve in tennis: effects of performance level. Medicine and Science in Sports and Exercise, 37, 1021-1029.

Goodwill, S.R., Chin, S.B., & Haake, S.J. (2004). Aerodynamics of spinning and non-spinning tennis balls. Journal of Wind Engineering and Industrial Aerodynamics, 92, 935-958.

Gordon, B.J. & Dapena, J. (2006). Contributions of joint rotations to racquet speed in the tennis serve. Journal of Sports Sciences, 24, 31-49.

Groppel, J.L. (1992). High Tech Tennis 2nd ed. Champaign, IL: Human Kinetics.

Groppel, J.L., Loehr, J.E., Melville, D.S., & Quinn, A.M. (1989). Science of Coaching Tennis. Champaign, IL: Human Kinetics.

Hreljac, A. (1998). Individual effects on biomechanical variables during landing in tennis shoes with varying midsole density. Journal of Sports Sciences, 16, 531-537.

Huches, M., & Meyers, R. (2005) Movement patterns in elite men's singles tennis. International Journal of Performance Analysis in Sport, 5(2), 110-134.

Iino, Y., & Kojima, T. (2003). Role of knee flexion and extension for rotating the trunk in a tennis forehand stroke. Journal of Human Movement Studies, 45, 133-152.

References

Kibler, W.B., Brody, H., Knudson, D., & Stroia, K. (2004). USTA Sport Science Committee White Paper on: Tennis Technique, Tennis Play, and Injury Prevention. Key Biscayne, FL: USTA.

Kibler, W.B., & Safran, M.R. (2000). Musculoskeletal injuries in the young tennis player. Clinics in Sports Medicine, 19, 781-792.

Knudson, D. (in press). Warm-up and flexibility. In: Chandler, J. & Brown, L.(Eds.). Introduction to Strength and Conditioning. Baltimore: Lippincott Williams & Wilkins.

Knudson, D. (2004). Biomechanical studies on the mechanism of tennis elbow. In M. Hubbard, R.D. Mehta, & J.M. Pallis (Eds.) The Engineering of Sport 5: Volume 1 (pp. 135-139). Sheffield: International Sports Engineering Association.

Knudson, D. (2003a). Fundamentals of Biomechanics. New York: Kluwer Academic-Plenum Publishers.

Knudson, D. (2003b) Stretching recommendations for tennis players. Medicine and Science in Tennis, 8 (3), 22-23.

Knudson, D. (1999). Using sport science to observe and correct tennis strokes. In B. Elliott, B. Gibson, and D. Knudson (Eds.) Applied Proceedings of the XVII International Symposium on Biomechanics in Sports, TENNIS. (pp. 7-16). Perth, Western Australia: Edith Cowan University.

Knudson, D. (1997). Effect of grip models on rebound accuracy of off-center tennis impacts. In J. Wilkerson, K. Ludwig, & W. Zimmerman (Eds.). Biomechanics in Sports XV: Proceedings of the 15th International Symposium on Biomechanics in Sports (pp. 483-487). Denton, TX: Texas Woman's University.

Knudson, D. (1990). Intra-subject variability of upper extremity angular kinematics in the tennis forehand drive. International Journal of Sport Biomechanics, 6, 415-421.

Knudson, D., & Bahamonde, R. (2001). Effect of endpoint conditions on position and velocity at impact in tennis. Journal of Sports Sciences, 19, 839-844.

Knudson, D., & Bahamonde, R. (1999). Trunk and racket kinematics at impact in the open and square stance tennis forehand. Biology of Sport, 16, 3-10.

Knudson, D., & Blackwell, J. (2005). Variability of impact kinematics and margin for error in the tennis forehand of advanced players. Sports Engineering, 8, 75-80.

Knudson, D., & Blackwell, J. (2001). Effect of type 3 ball on upper extremity EMG and acceleration in the tennis forehand. In J.R. Blackwell (Ed.) Proceedings of Oral Sessions: XIX International Symposium on Biomechanics in Sports. (pp. 32-34). San Francisco, CA: University of San Francisco.

Knudson, D., & Blackwell, J. (1997). Upper extremity angular kinematics of the one-handed backhand drive in tennis players with and without tennis elbow. International Journal of Sports Medicine, 18, 79-82.

Knudson, D., & Elliott, B.C. (2004). Biomechanics of tennis strokes. In: G.K. Hung & J.M. Pallis (Eds.). Biomedical Engineering Principles in Sports. (pp. 153-181). New York: Kluwer Academic/Plenum Publishers.

Knudson, D., & Elliott, B.C. (2003). Analysis of advanced stroke production. In: B. Elliott, M. Reid, & M. Crespo (Eds). Biomechanics of Advanced Tennis Coaching. (pp. 137-154). London: International Tennis Federation.

Knudson, D., Magnusson, S.P., & McHugh, M. 2000, June). Current issues in flexibility fitness. President's Council on Physical Fitness and Sports Research Digest. 1-8.

Knudson, D., & Morrison, C. (2002). Qualitative analysis of human movement 2nd ed. Champaign, IL: Human Kinetics.

Knudson, D., & Shriver, P. (2001). Self-Analysis. In: P. Roetert, & J. Groppel (Eds). World-Class Tennis Technique. (pp. 247-262). Champaign, IL: Human Kinetics.

Kraemer, W.J. et al. (2003). Physiological changes with periodized resistance training in women tennis players. Medicine and Science in Sports and Exercise, 35, 157-168.

Kraemer, W.J. et al. (2000). Influence of resistance training volume and periodization on physiological and performance adaptations in college women tennis players. American Journal of Sports Medicine, 28, 626-633.

Lamond, F., Lowdon, B., & Davis, K. (1996). Determination of the quickest footwork for teaching return of the tennis serve. ACHPER Healthy Lifestyles Journal, 43(3), 5-8.

Li, F.X, Fewtrell, D., & Jenkins, M. (2004). String vibration dampers do not reduce racket frame vibration transfer to the forearm. Journal of Sports Science, 22, 1041-1052.

Lo, K., Wang, L., Wu, C., Su, F. (2004). Biomechanical analysis of trunk and lower extremity in the tennis serve. In: Lamontagne, M., Robertson, D., & Sveistrup, H. (Eds). Proceedings of the XXII International Symposium of Biomechanics in Sport (pp. 261-264). Ottawa: University of Ottawa.

Maffulli, N., Wong, J. & Almekinders, L.C. (2003). Types and epidemiology of tendinopathy. Clinics in Sports Medicine, 22, 675-692.

Metha, R., & Pallis, J. (2001). The aerodynamics of a tennis ball. Sports Engineering, 4, 177-189.

Nigg, B.M., Luthi, S.M., & Bahlsen, H.A. (1989). The tennis shoe-biomechanical design criteria. In: Segesser, B., & Pforringer, W. (Eds). The Shoe in Sport (pp. 39-46). New York: Year Book Medical Publishers.

Nigg, B.N., & Segesser, B. (1988). The influence of playing surfaces on the load on the locomotor system and on football and tennis injuries. Sports Medicine, 5, 375-385.

Pallis, J.M. et al. (1997). Tennis Sport Science. http://wings.avkids.com/Tennis/ (accessed January 5, 2005).

Plagenhoef, S. (1979). Tennis racket testing related to tennis elbow. In: J. Groppel (Ed). A National Symposium on the Racket Sports (pp. 291-310). Urbana-Champaign, IL: University of Illinois Press.

Plagenhoef, S. (1970). Fundamentals of Tennis. Englewood Cliffs, NJ: Prentice-Hall.

Pluim, B., & Safran, M. (2004) From Breakpoint to Advantage. Vista, CA: Racquet Tech Publishing.

References

Priest, J.D., & Nagle, D.A. (1976). Tennis shoulder. American Journal of Sports Medicine, 4, 28-42.

Reid, M., & Elliott, B. (2002). The one- and two-handed backhands in tennis. Sports Biomechanics, 1, 47-68.

Reid, M., Quinn, A., & Crespo, M. (Eds). (2003). Strength and Conditioning for Tennis. London: International Tennis Federation.

Roetert, E., & Ellenbecker, T. (Eds). (2002). Complete Conditioning for Tennis. Champaign, IL: Human Kinetics.

Roetert, P., & Groppel, J. (Eds). (2001). World-Class Tennis Technique. Champaign, IL: Human Kinetics.

Shapriro, R., Uhl, T., Seeley, M., McGinn, P., McCrory, J., & Kibler, W.B. (submitted). Biomechanical comparison of the traditional serve and the abbreviated serve.

Shim, J., Carlton, L.G., Chow, J.W., & Chae, W. (2005). The use of anticipatory cues by highly skilled tennis players. Journal of Motor Behavior, 37, 164-175.

Sprigings, E., Marshall, R., Elliott, B., & Jennings, L. (1994). A three-dimensional kinematic method for determining the effectiveness of arm segment rotations in producing racquet-had speed. Journal of Biomechanics, 27, 245-254.

Stroede, C.L., Noble, L., & Walker, H.S. (1999). The effects of tennis racket string vibration dampers on racket handle vibrations and discomfort following impacts. Journal of Sports Sciences, 17, 379-385.

Stussi, A., Stacoff, A., & Tiegermann, V. (1989). Rapid sideward movements in tennis. In: Segesser, B., & Pforringer, W. (Eds). The Shoe in Sport (pp. 53-62). New York: Year Book Medical Publishers.

Takahashi, K., Elliott, B., & Noffal, G. (1996). The role of upper limb segment rotations in the development of spin in the tennis forehand. Australian Journal of Science and Medicine in Sport, 28, 106-113.

United States Tennis Association (2004). Dynamic Tennis Warm-ups [DVD]. Champaign, IL: Human Kinetics.

Vad, V.B. et al. (2003). Hip and shoulder internal rotation range of motion deficits in professional tennis players. Journal of Science and Medicine in Sport, 6, 71-75.

Van Gheluwe, B., & Hebbelinck, M. (1986). The kinematics of the volley movement in tennis: a three-dimensional cinematographical approach. In: Biomechanics: 1984 Olympic Scientific Congress Proceedings (pp. 101-110). Colorado Springs, CO: USOC.

Van Gheluwe, B., de Ruysscher, & Craenhals, J. (1987). Pronation and endorotation of the racket arm in a tennis serve. In: Jonsson (Ed). Biomechanics X-B (pp. 667-672). Champaign, IL: Human Kinetics.

Walther, M., Kirschner, S., Koenig, A., Barthel, T., & Gohlke, F. (2002) Biomechanical evaluation of braces used for the treatment of epicondylitis. Journal of Shoulder and Elbow Surgery, 11, 265-270.

Wang, L.H., Wu, C., & Su, F. (2002). Three-dimensional kinematics of the upper extremity in the tennis volley. In S. Ujihashi, & S.J. Haake (Eds.), The Engineering of Sport 4 (pp. 725-729). Oxford: Blackwell Science.

Wang, L.H., Wu, C.C., Su, F.C., Lo, K., & Wu, H. (2000). Kinematics of the trunk and upper extremity in tennis flat serve. In S.J. Haake, & A. Coe (Eds.), Tennis Science and Technology (pp. 395-400). Oxford: Blackwell Science.

Waugh, E.J. (2005). Lateral epicondylalgia or epicondylitis: what's in a name? Journal of Orthopaedic and Sports Physical Therapy, 35, 200-201.

Williams, A.M., Ward, P., Knowles, J.M., & Smeeton, N.J. (2002). Anticipation skills in a real-world task: measurement, training, and transfer in tennis. Journal of Experimental Psychology: Applied, 8, 259-270.

Yuan, J., Wang, M., & Murrell, G.A.C. (2003). Cell death and tendinopathy. Clinics in Sports Medicine, 22, 693-701.

Zajac, F.E., Neptune, R.R., & Kautz, S.A. (2002). Biomechanics and muscle coordination of human walking part I: introduction to concepts, power transfer, dynamics and simulations. Gait and Posture, 16, 215-232.

Zajac, F.E., & Gordon, M.E. (1989). Determining muscle's force and action in multi-aticular movement. Exercise and Sport Sciences Reviews, 17, 187-230.

Index

Index

Index

in linked-segment system,
10–11, 55f
principles of, 9b
Twist serve
advantages of, 68
arm motions for, 68–69,
72
bounce of, 68
Coordination and Transfer
of Energy Principle
applied to, 68–69, 72
description of, 32
illustration of, 33f
racquet motion in, 72
summary of, 72
topspin of, 68
toss for, 54
Two-handed backhand
coordination used in, 102,
102f–103f
description of, 24, 27
disguise advantages of,
103
follow-through in, 104, 110
footwork for, 98
grip for, 96–97
joint motions used in, 101
one-handed backhand vs.,
101, 104b
preparation for, 98
stroke for, 101–103
summary of, 110
technique for, 106b–107b

V

Viscoelasticity, 56, 56b
Vision, 114b–115b
Volley
backswing of, 122b–123b
cross-over step for,
112–113, 113f
description of, 111
down-the-line, 112, 117,
118f
drive, 119f, 119–120
drop, 120
footwork for, 112–113

grips for, 111–112
margin for error in,
120–121
Optimal Projection
Principle for, 120–121
preparation for, 112–113
punch, 113–117,
119–120
reaction times,
114b–115b
stroke used in, 113, 115
summary of, 121, 124
swing, 118b
technique for, 122b–123b
vision during, 114b–115b

W

Warm-up, 28–29
Weight training, 27
Western grip, 76f, 76–77
Wrist extensor muscle, 26
Wrist hyperextension, 99,
100f
Wrist snap, 60–62